Getting the Buggers Excited about ICT

Also available from Continuum

Dyslexia in the Digital Age, Ian Smythe
Homo Zappiens, Wim Veen & Ben Vrakking
Innovate with ICT, Johannes Ahrenfelt & Neal Watkin
Teaching Mathematics Using ICT, Adrian Oldknow, Ron
    Taylor & Linda Tetlow
Teaching English Using ICT, Tom Rank, Chris Warren &
    Trevor Millum

Getting the Buggers Excited about ICT

KAREN ANDERSON

continuum

A companion website to accompany this book is available online at: http://education.anderson.continuumbooks.com

Please visit the link and register with us to receive your password and to access these downloadable resources.

If you experience any problems accessing the resources, please contact Continuum at: info@continuumbooks.com

Continuum International Publishing Group

The Tower Building   80 Maiden Lane
11 York Road   Suite 704
London SE1 7NX   New York NY 10038

www.continuumbooks.com

British Library Cataloguing-in-Publication Data
A catalogue record for this book is available from the British Library.

ISBN: 978-1-4411-9855-6 (paperback)

Library of Congress Cataloging-in-Publication Data
Anderson, Karen, 1981-
Getting the buggers excited about ICT / Karen Anderson.
p. cm.
Includes index.
ISBN 978-1-4411-9855-6 (pbk.)
1. Computer-assisted instruction. 2. Educational technology. 3. Education—Effect of technological innovations on I. Title.

LB1028.5.A464 2010
371.33′4—dc22   2010020556

Typeset by Pindar NZ, Auckland, New Zealand
Printed and bound in Great Britain by the MPG Books Group

Contents

Contents

List of Activities

- ➡️ – Lesson Activity
- 🕐 – approximate duration
- ⚡ – instant activity
- 👥 – pair activity
- 👪 – group activity
- 👨‍👩‍👧 – class activity
- ⇨ – extend this activity

The basics

Skills-based ICT

Problem-solving ICT

Multimedia

Teaching ICT without a computer

Extra-curricular activities

Online Lesson Activities

File Types Bingo
My Documents Folder
Carbon Copies
To Reply or Not To Reply
Risk Assess Your ICT Room
Censorship
Panel Debate (aka Question Time)
Battleships
Human Formulae
Formulae with Cards
Relationships in Databases
Normalization
Entity Relationship Diagrams (ERDs)
Organizing a Party

Introduction

ICT, in my opinion, is the most exciting subject. It's invigorating to teach and enjoyable to learn. It never gets stagnant; it is always changing and never gets boring. It is something that can be taught with a lot of freedom, with creativity and with the chance to do something different – going off-brief sometimes produces better results, and individuality can be encouraged. Also there is the other side of ICT: the logical, mathematical, precise side which encourages us to be highly accurate and disciplined. By using these two very different approaches, by employing both sides of the brain simultaneously, ICT can be completely engaging for both you and your pupils. How many other subjects can say with near certainty that when the pupils they teach go home 100 per cent will continue doing their subject. It may not be academic work, but if they are surfing the net, emailing, chatting on social networking, playing a computer game or making a movie they are doing ICT and it all benefits their learning in your subject.

ICT affects everyone, in both personal and professional lives, and no matter what your pupils will do in the future, they need this subject. All young people must be ICT literate in order for them to survive and be successful in our modern world. It is not just an important skill to have: it is one which is expected. Applicants to university must demonstrate they have ICT skills; job applications expect ICT skills to be included as standard and as such ICT has become a staple of the school and college curriculum. It is the route to learning, employment, friendships – our society revolves around technology.

Our young people are 'digital natives'; they have grown up surrounded by technology from before they can remember and feel comfortable with it. I have heard intelligent people with degrees, masters and doctorates describing how they had to ask their 10-year-old son, daughter, nephew or niece to install some software, record a programme from television or how their children had saved them from calling out a costly engineer.

However, there are many preconceptions and misconceptions about teaching ICT, which makes it a very misunderstood subject. There are also barriers that deter teachers from approaching it creatively, using it in a cross-curricular way or pushing the boundaries of the subject – or even getting anywhere near the boundaries!

There is a shortage of ICT teachers, there probably always will be. Unlike other academic areas, you don't find many people taking an ICT or Computing degree with the end goal of becoming a teacher. They aspire to be computer games programmers, network administrators and telecommunications engineers – they are looking for very technical, highly paid jobs. A high proportion of ICT teachers either 'fell into' the job or studied to teach in a subject such as Maths or Business and started teaching ICT because they were unable to get teaching positions in their own subjects, or there was a gap in their school and they volunteered to fill it. This means you will most likely be able to identify yourself as being in one of these main categories:

-   those who are ICT experts, trained in ICT and education and want to be ICT teachers
-   those who are ICT experts but not teachers, meaning they have a wealth of subject knowledge but are maybe unsure of how to deliver this knowledge or make it engaging
-   those who are teachers, but not ICT experts, with excellent teaching skills, but unsure about the subject content and how to deliver it, as ICT delivery is very different to all other subjects.

However, it doesn't matter how you got into ICT teaching or what type of ICT teacher you are – you will never regret it.

How to use this book

This book addresses issues that often arise within the teaching of ICT, and provides practical ideas that can be used in the classroom, including:

-   discrete ICT – the teaching of ICT as a subject in its own right
-   cross-curricular ICT – using ICT in other subjects and across the school. This is something which is an expectation in schools and will be examined in inspections; it led Ofsted (Office for Standards in

Education) to publish the report *The Importance of ICT* on their website in 2009, an interesting overview of ICT in UK schools.

It also looks at pupils using ICT at home and in their leisure time, and how that can help them and you. As an ICT teacher, you will be involved in eSafety, possibly even responsible for it throughout the school, and this is covered in this book. Finally, there is a look at going further, pushing your pupils and extending their learning, involvement and participation.

As a full-time teacher myself I understand that you do not have much free time and I have made this book as accessible as possible and not a chore to read, providing practical ideas and advice that you can take straight into the classroom. You may wish to read it through or dip into for reference when you need it – I hope you find it suitable for both.

You will also find references to resources on this book's companion website throughout. The web address is:

http://education.anderson.continuumbooks.com

On the companion website you will be able to find up-to-date information, links to useful websites, further lesson ideas and activity resources already prepared for you to use in your lessons.

The 'ICT – that's easy to teach' myth

Is this scenario familiar to you?

[Location – conference, party or other social gathering]

Person A:	What do you do?
Me:	I'm a teacher.
Person A:	*(looking impressed)* Teaching, that's a hard job. What subject?
Me:	ICT
Person A:	*(looking less impressed)* Well, that must be easy, all young people love computers.

This is the point at which I want to jump on the nearest table and scream at the top of my voice:

No! I love my subject but it is *not* easy and just because young people like using computers for surfing the internet and chatting with their friends does not mean they automatically enjoy studying ICT. Do you know any young person who enjoys spreadsheets or the Data Protection Act?!

At this point I would probably be carted away by the men in white coats, so I've resisted actually saying all this out loud.

I find it incredibly frustrating that there is a view that ICT is 'easy' to teach, that all young people can already use it well, that it's not a 'proper' subject. I have seen schools who have pupils who cannot pass other qualifications put into GCSE ICT classes because 'at least they'll get one GCSE' – and then they're surprised when these pupils fail this subject as well. That's because ICT is not the easy option; it's not there as a safety net for weak pupils. It is equal to all other subjects.

Perhaps this illusion originates from pupils who are evidently weak in other subjects being seen to perform well in ICT. This is not because it is the easy option; it is because its practical nature suits some pupils better than other subjects, although it is still equally academically rigorous. If ICT is run as a vocational subject, it can suit those pupils who are not natural academics, those who find it difficult to write long essays. It is not the easy option, but gives a positive alternative to other academic qualifications such as GCSEs and A-levels; a different approach but still on the same level of attainment.

Consider some of the differences between the challenge of teaching ICT and History, a more 'academic' subject, as shown in the Table 1.

Table 1

History	ICT
A history textbook will always work, it will always open, the text will always be there on the pages.	When an ICT teacher walks into an ICT room to teach a lesson, there is always the possibility of some or all of the computers not working. No matter how good your IT Support is, sometimes computers fail or there might be a power cut. It is something we must be ready for, an extra consideration when planning our lessons.
History textbooks will only be used for studying History and usually only during lessons or other study times.	Schools often have an open ICT room policy for pupils to have access in their free time (which is fantastic); however, it can result in problems occurring outside lesson time or leave problems for when lessons resume in that room.
The Nazis will always lose World War II, King Henry VIII will always have six wives, etc.	Software changes regularly, whether a small update, full rebuild or the software is discontinued and an alternative has to be found. All elements of ICT go out of date so quickly that generally ICT teachers need to rewrite some or all of their teaching materials every year.

ICT is suffering from an identity crisis. It is a practical subject which has theoretical foundations. There is a struggle, especially when exam boards need to devise qualifications, to decide what to assess and how to create a balance. The people who make these decisions are asking themselves:

> Do we only look at their practical abilities, e.g. can they use a computer to produce the desired result; if so, how do we measure that? Are we to assess their understanding? Should ICT be an examined subject? Can written exams really assess someone's ability to use ICT? Can a practical exam within a short time limit truly assess a user's ability? Can a longer practical exam, over days or months, be proven to be the candidate's own work? Can we justify assessing pupils individually in ICT when teamwork is such a large part of it in the real world? Should learners be allowed to use the internet to find answers when being assessed? After all they would have it in the real world . . .

As you can see, it is a thorny problem and one which is still very much being debated by education professionals.

Assessment methods range from peculiar (written questions *about* spreadsheets, rather than *making* a spreadsheet) to overkill (taking hundreds of screenshots). There is sometimes a disparity between the time taken to create a product and the time taken to provide the materials for assessment. For example, a pupil who has learned how to make databases could create one in a few hours, yet the paperwork which has to go with it could take weeks.

Does this all sound confusing and like ICT is a difficult subject? Are you regretting choosing ICT as your teaching subject? Are you wondering how much French you actually remember from school and whether it would be easier to teach that?

Do not worry.

There are many issues and debates around ICT, but that actually makes things better for you and your pupils. It means you have more freedom. There is no set way to teach ICT, therefore you can carve your own path. There is a plethora of qualifications available to study in ICT: due to the uncertainty of the assessment of the subject, exam boards have created qualifications which cover just about everything. You could go general or specific; academic or vocational; or applied (a bit of both); you could deliver it discretely, across the curriculum, in an extra-curricular capacity, or use a combination of all these methods.

Consider some of the positive differences between teaching ICT and History, a more 'academic' subject, as shown in Table 2.

Table 2

History	ICT
There are standard textbooks which are used in History, ones which are recommended and expected; they all cover the same material as History does not change.	In teaching ICT, you have the freedom to choose your software, even your operating system and platform. Although there is an expectation of Microsoft products, there is no rule that says you have to use those and exam boards cannot penalize you for using something else. You could even use entirely freeware and GPL software – your school's Finance department will love you for that!
History textbooks will only be used for studying History and usually only during lessons or other study times.	Isn't it great that pupils will want to use the equipment from your lesson in their free time? Half the battle is already won.
The Nazis will always lose World War II, King Henry VIII will always have six wives, etc.	When I was in school, I used to wonder how teachers did not get bored teaching the same thing over and over again – ICT is anything but boring!

Believe me, as one ICT teacher to another, you have made the right choice in choosing ICT.

Breaking the barriers to ICT

ICT as a subject in education can be daunting and there are many perceived barriers. However, with research, determination and a little lateral thinking, all can be overcome.

'ICT is expensive, my school can't afford loads of fancy equipment'

The expense of ICT equipment can be one of the biggest deterrents to innovative ICT in schools. The latest hardware is released at extraordinarily high prices, industry-standard software is phenomenally expensive and exciting equipment such as video cameras and games consoles are barely even considered because of the cost. Although schools are generally willing to invest in ICT, there is always a limit and budgets will only stretch so far. Also you may find it hard to justify replacing something which you have only been using for a year or two, even though that's how fast technology moves.

However, you do not have to use the latest hardware and software to produce amazing results. For example, when buying digital cameras, find the one you would ideally wish to buy and see if the model just below it will do what you need without the bells and whistles of the more expensive one. Watch out for discontinued lines and make use of bulk buying. Never be scared to call up a company and negotiate, stressing the fact that you are using their products to educate the leaders of tomorrow – pull on the heart strings if necessary.

Consider freeware and GPL software, all of which is free, and usually able to be used across your network. There are usually free versions of any software you would need to use, even of the big, very expensive packages (see this book's companion website for suggestions). Although they may not have all the functionality of the larger products, really consider what you actually need. Will your pupils make use of all the tools, or will a cut-down version actually help them and remove the intimidation factor of the larger product?

If you need to buy expensive products, think about how you might negotiate the deal. For example, offer to be involved in their advertising as a case study to entice more schools to purchase it, or even consider offering to advertise the company in your school by, for example, putting the logo on all project booklets used by pupils in the ICT department.

'Everything in ICT changes too quickly'

The speed at which ICT changes can be intimidating. It almost seems as though just as you have got one thing purchased, installed and being used it is superseded by something else. Do not be put off by this. You do not need to use the latest gadgets in your lessons. Although you must make sure you do not get left behind, don't feel you need to jump every time something new is released. Keep up to date with new technology by reading magazines, such as *Computer Weekly*, *Wired* (for developments in technology), *.net* (for internet), *Edge* (for computer games), *Computer Arts* (for multimedia) and blogs, and by watching for announcements from the major companies.

Pupils and parents might ask you about new technology, but be prepared with your answers. For example, the week when Windows Vista was released my pupils were constantly asking me when we were going to upgrade, but I had my answer ready and explained to them how big our network was, how we needed to make sure it was stable and what the consequences of rushing into it would be – by explaining it to them, they understood and soon the questions stopped. Also consider having a display in your classroom and inviting your pupils to add 'the latest thing' to it, a big picture of it with pros and cons – it allows those who are interested to produce a display for all pupils to see, they have to rationalize it with positives and negatives, and it is there for other pupils to see as well.

As an ICT teacher, you have to accept that your curriculum will change more often than others. It is inevitable and, if you think about it objectively, wholly right that your subject should move with the times. Be prepared for qualifications to only last three years before being radically changed, and also keep an eye on exam board websites for sudden changes, as they do happen every now and again.

Although you may need to be more flexible than other teachers, remember that every time there are changes it allows you to reflect on what has gone before and continually improve. It provides the opportunity to try new approaches, to add a bit of pizzazz to something which may have turned out a little dry, to experiment with new ideas. If you find your subject exciting and varied so will your pupils and they will be more engaged.

'I do what I've always done because it works'

Pupils are changing – I don't mean they are mutating into monsters, but the way they learn is changing. The 'old style' learner would expect to work by themselves, using the materials the teacher had provided, and generally carry out one task at a time. The 'new model' learner has grown up in a digital age and has a different approach to their learning. They will look for opportunities to collaborate with work (not copy, but genuinely work with, others), they will consider the material from the teacher and then do further research on the internet and find multi-tasking a natural process. For more detail on this, see the section on digital natives and digital immigrants in Chapter 6 (page 149).

This change in learners is most clearly evident in ICT. They will enter your school with an increasing amount of ICT knowledge and ability to do all sorts of things that you would normally have had to teach them. It would be easy to 'do what you have always done', but there is a chance you could disengage your pupils, especially those who are new to the school and at their most keen and receptive stage. By adjusting your teaching style and content to match your pupils, you will find they are more engaged and they will find lessons more interesting and both of you will benefit. Although this will mean more preparation, it will mean better, more meaningful, more productive lessons.

'I don't have time to create innovative lessons because I'm asked to do all sorts of other things'

As an ICT teacher, you may have obligations which equivalent teachers in other subjects do not have. For example, you may be responsible for eSafety, looking after a VLE (virtual learning environment), preparing ICT resources for other subjects, training staff in ICT, cross-curricular ICT, working with the IT Support department. You may be stopped in the corridor to be asked about a jammed printer, a faulty laptop or someone's computer at home that's stopped working.

You need to be careful about managing your workload. You need to be assertive and learn to say 'No' very politely. (Admittedly, I speak as one who is still learning that one.) If you feel your workload is too much, speak to someone – your head of department, your senior management – there is always something that can be done to help you out.

Consider creative approaches to some of your tasks such as:

- setting up an extra-curricular group for pupils to create resources for your VLE or for other subjects, which benefits both you and them
- creating a core group of eager ICT enthusiasts on the staff whom you can train and then they can disseminate it around the school, rather than you trying to reach everyone
- getting your IT Support team on board and discussing issues with them – they may come up with some exciting ideas for you, approaching topics from a non-teaching perspective.

There are lots of creative ideas in this book for lessons and activities which may give you the confidence to take a different approach, get others involved and even simplify your teaching.

'They need to learn how to use the software, I don't have time for anything else'

There is a lot to fit into an ICT curriculum. Where you might be required to teach pupils 'to use a SUM function in a spreadsheet', getting them to the point where they can do that can take several lessons. They may need to learn how to input data, how to format cells, how to do formulae, and so on. Unlike learning facts, there is a cumulative approach needed within a topic. You may find a lot of your time is spent teaching your pupils how to use software and then getting them to fulfil the criteria. For a really squashed timetable, you may find yourself teaching to use the software *while* they are fulfilling the criteria. Even though you may want to do more with them and give them more independence and stretch them, you may find your time limited and you have to just 'bomb through' the material.

Consider other approaches. Can you give learning-the-software tasks for homework, for example could you give them exercises or instructions to carry out in preparation for the next lesson where they will use that learning from the homework independently? This is actually a very old idea, of having 'prep' or preparation so they are ready for the next lesson. Can you team up with a colleague to deliver some of your material? For example, if you teach your pupils to make and use spreadsheets, could they then use that learning to analyse data collected from their Science experiments – both subjects will benefit and the pupils see their ICT knowledge being put to a practical application. Might you be able to encourage extra work outside the classroom to extend their learning – in competitions, extra-curricular projects or independent extension work? If you want to push your pupils, if you want to further their learning but find yourself short of contact time with them, consider ways of doing it without you needing to be present where they can take everything they have learned from you and apply it themselves.

'I don't know how to manage a lesson in an ICT room'

If you are not familiar with teaching in an ICT room, they can be daunting places. Unlike 'normal' classrooms where the pupils are generally facing the front, in ICT rooms they can be facing all sorts of directions, even with their backs to you, and with a variety of distractions available to them on the internet. You may be worried the pupils will try to get away with misbehaviour or pull the wool over your eyes if you have a lack of ICT knowledge. However, with preparation, positivity and practice, you will find an ICT room quickly changes from a intimidating place to an inviting place. See the section 'Managing an ICT Lesson' on page 100.

'I'm not an ICT expert – I can only teach them the basics'

Do not be intimidated by your pupils' ICT knowledge. Even if you are an ICT expert, there will still be areas you are a bit shaky on. And, believe me, there will always be one pupil in all of your classes who knows more than you do. That's fine. Allow them to be 'your expert', allow them to help you, to show you how to do something. Don't push them down, raise them up and get your pupils to aspire to be 'your expert'. If you hide that you do not know something, your pupils will spot it immediately and you will lose their trust – if you lie and say you know something when you don't, it could damage your relationship with them. Be honest and say that you are not sure, but you will look it up. Do so and come back to the next lesson armed with the information and impress them that you remembered their question and have taken the time to find out for them. They will appreciate that.

You will see symbols in the text, pointing out certain items:

 These are key points, usually focused on pedagogy or teaching in general, which are fundamental for you as a teacher of ICT.

 This icon flags up issues which need to be considered or will help you avoid potential common pitfalls.

1

ICT as a Discrete Subject

By choosing ICT, you have opted to teach the best subject available. I'm sure all teachers would say their subject is the best, but let me explain why yours is truly the best:

1　You are teaching a subject where genuinely all students have the potential to get the top grade, be that A*, Distinction or otherwise. I have not met a student yet who *couldn't* achieve the highest grade in ICT. It purely depends on how enthusiastic you make them, how much hard work they put in, and their willingness to follow your instructions. When I meet new classes for the first time, I often start by telling them they can all achieve the highest grade and I genuinely mean that – and I go on to tell them how to do it: work hard and enjoy it; the rest will happen along the journey.

2　You will become revered by other teachers because you understand computers, those strange, mystical boxes that they all have to have in their classrooms now. This will increase exponentially if you are inclined to help them every now and again, showing how to organise their emails or unjamming a printer.

3　You have a whole-school view. Nearly all subjects are quite entrenched in their own departments, whereas ICT *has* to consider the needs of the whole school. Your perspective is quite different to other teachers' and therefore you can find yourself in important discussions about, say, the direction of the school, or being involved in a list of interesting projects which look fantastic on your CV should you wish to seek promotion.

4　You will never get bored teaching ICT. You will always have another approach to try, another piece of software to switch to or an extra thing you can show your students or colleagues.

5　You can learn from your students. There will be many times when you explain how to do something and a little voice from the back will say,

'There's a better way to do it . . .', or you will be asked something and before you can reply, another student will step in and demonstrate. You may find yourself looking at a student's work and wondering how they achieved it technically. Don't be scared of this, don't think it is showing you up or highlighting any sort of lack of knowledge. Embrace this. It means that your students are engaged and learning. Praise this enthusiasm and innovation – and learn from your students.

Teaching is the best job in the world – and in selecting ICT as your subject you have chosen wisely. Whether it was always your desire to do this or you have stumbled upon it, I hope you never regret reaching the point you are at at this very moment. Every time you stand in front of your students, remember the importance of what you are doing, that you are giving them a gift, an opportunity to build a bright future for themselves.

ICT: The subject

ICT is taught in all schools usually as a core subject, one which all students will need for their futures, along with English and Maths. However, it is a relatively young subject, having been a core subject in schools for a relatively short period of time. Unlike more established subjects, it is still finding its feet and is approached in many different ways. Some schools may take the academic route and run the GCSE qualification, others may opt for more vocational qualifications, while many will have a mixture of both and also cover Functional Skills. Students may have a choice of course they sit, or the school may decide that all will sit the same qualification. At Level 3, there is a huge range of qualifications available: academic, vocational and mixed; general and specialist – worth from one A-level to three A-levels. This wide range at both Level 2 and Level 3 can allow students' education to be tailored towards their interests and futures.

Having this huge range of qualifications, directions and opportunities can make things tricky for teachers of ICT. All subjects are wide-ranging, but generally focus on specific topics, whereas for ICT it seems depth can often be sacrificed for breadth, giving students a taste of all areas, from databases to web design, programming to animation, and even touching on other subjects including Business and Media. How can a teacher manage this? There are two approaches you could take.

1 teach with as much depth as possible, giving students as much as possible in the time you have, although you may find yourself really

pushing it and struggling to fit everything in. You will be giving your students everything they could possibly need, and you are giving it to all of them, not missing any out.

2 Alternatively, accept the 'breadth-over-depth' principle and give students a taster of as many areas as possible. If you make it exciting, hopefully you will encourage them to continue their studies in their own time, to choose to do it, and even to enjoy their homework. Think of yourself as sowing the seeds and your students as tending and nurturing them. With this approach you have less control and not all students will take what you have given and make it grow. However, those who do take the opportunity you've given them will set down roots in the subject more firmly.

You will find students having very differing abilities in ICT: some may never have used anything like it; some may be very competent. This is the nature of the subject – because students use it to varying degrees outside lessons, you need to be prepared for a very wide level of differentiation, unusually based on experience rather than ability. It is an exciting challenge to ensure those with little ICT knowledge are given all the basic skills they need, without allowing those who are already adept to become bored.

I find introducing a spirit of co-operation and assistance works well. Often if I have shown one student how to do something, when someone else in the class asks exactly the same thing, I will ask the first student to show the second. This not only allows me to move on and help someone else, rather than repeating the same thing, but also reinforces the learning of the first student and proves they have understood my explanation. Also, students often learn ideas better when told by their peers rather than by their teacher. I always frame the request positively and politely: 'Sally, you've just made a great job of turning your page landscape – would you mind showing Charlie? I'm sure he'd appreciate your help.' Adding the last sentence to the request can bolster the student's confidence that they *will* be able to help the other student. This works especially well for students who are weaker and allows them to show others in the group that they have mastered a technique before others.

The same issue can arise when putting students into pairs or groups, an incredibly useful approach in ICT, which lends itself to co-operative and collaborative learning easily. It can be useful to know your students' level of expertise or confidence in a topic beforehand so as to match them up more appropriately. Allowing students to organize themselves can work well if you want them to pair up with friends; however, if you want an even spread of skills, you need to be more tactful.

You could introduce your class to a 'confidence count'. After introducing a topic, the teacher asks, 'How confident do you feel about this topic?' and the students' response is to raise their hands, showing the number of fingers appropriate to their level of confidence: 0 for 'Really not sure', 5 for 'Could happily do this task by myself'.

If the confidence count is introduced early on, when most students will be confident about the topics covered, they will feel more secure in using it later when the topics become more challenging. If weaker students see others with low numbers of fingers, it can show them that they are not alone in lacking understanding. Alternatively, you could ask them to do this with eyes closed, although someone is always bound to peek!

You can then use this confidence count to create interesting pairings. Don't make the difference between pairings too great, e.g. 5s with 0s will find each other frustrating. Try 0s with 3s, 1s with 4s and 2s with 5s.

This can also be used as a plenary to assess the learning which has taken place – hopefully you should see more fingers raised at the end than at the beginning!

An alternative to this could be to write the number on a piece of paper and hold it up, or use some other sort of indicator – perhaps red, yellow and green Lego bricks for a traffic-light system.

There are commonalities between all areas of ICT, whether you are focusing on something very technical or on a more creative aspect. In terms of the work, you will find the Systems Life Cycle cropping up again and again in specifications, which is so crucial to ICT – the day it disappears from specs will be because it is so ingrained in the subject that it no longer has to be considered as a separate entity. For everything that is done in ICT, even at a basic level, the Systems Life Cycle should contain these components: Planning, Implementation, Testing, Evaluation. No matter what your students are creating, these are the key steps that should always occur.

As for the concept, there is a key commonality which should always exist and be fundamental to ICT projects: that it is useful and valuable. You should be able to justify why your students are learning about each part of the curriculum – even legislation. Try to place all of your work in a real-world context and demonstrate the importance of them knowing and understanding it. They *will* be using it in their futures.

There are two rationales for students deciding to study ICT and all students will fall into one of these categories:

- **ICT as a function:** All students in their futures, no matter what they do, will be involved in using computers in some way. An ICT qualification which is general and covers areas such as word processing, presentations, spreadsheets, databases and a little multimedia will give these students enough knowledge and practical skills to become confident users of ICT. By analogy, they are like the majority of people who drive a car – they know how to operate it to get from A to B, without ever wanting to lift the bonnet and find out why it works.

– **ICT as a career:** An increasing number of students will go on to study ICT and its various specialisms after school and these are the students who need to take more in-depth qualifications. They may start on general ICT qualifications, covering the breadth of the subject, perhaps discovering their interest there, or perhaps it is an interest they have developed at home; they will eventually move on to a specialist course at degree level or a trainee position in employment. These are the people who do open the bonnet and discover the wonders hidden underneath. Their specialisms can range from hardware, networking, programming, multimedia – and the further a student progresses with their ICT, the more specific their courses can become, such as systems support or computer games design.

Whichever path is chosen, ICT is a compulsory component of the National Curriculum from Key Stage 1 (ages 5–7) right up to Key Stage 4 (ages 14–16). Even if a qualification is not offered or taken at Key Stage 4, schools must still provide a programme of study for ICT and is a core subject. This chapter will discuss these areas and give practical ideas and lesson plans which you can take straight into the classroom.

> When I was training, a mentor said to me: 'You can't please all of the students, all of the time.' That was an excellent piece of advice and one which is so true. You will never have a whole class fascinated in each project you do. Your aim is to get the majority interested and all of them doing it.

The basics

There are fundamentals of ICT which all students should have an under-standing of, whether they plan to study it further or not. These basics will prove useful when using ICT in both their careers and their personal lives. The teaching of these topics, however, is sometimes skipped or rushed;

17

they are seen as obvious or it is assumed students will already know about them. Sometimes it is the dullness of the topic, for example legislation, which causes it to be skimmed quickly. Yet these basics are fundamental to your students' understanding of ICT and will help them later when they are carrying out more advanced tasks and using software.

Some of these topics are best introduced as early as possible, such as email and searching for information on the internet, whereas others can be included at any point. Each of the following Lesson Activities stands alone, and therefore can be used as ice-breakers at the start of a term to get students focused before starting a larger project. They can also be put in at the end of a project or just before the school breaks up for a holiday, or even used in the middle of a project to give students a short break before returning to the larger piece of work. Include and use these activities in the way that best suits your teaching, students and scheme of work.

Hardware and components

A good place to start with ICT education is understanding all the parts of a computer and the peripherals and media which can be used. This is often overlooked as teachers can assume that students will already know this; however, it is a good opportunity to iron out any misconceptions, demonstrate to less confident students that they do have some ICT knowledge, and push them a little further by introducing equipment they may not have seen before.

> ⚿ Part of becoming an effective user of ICT involves being confident about using a computer. A good way to do this is to remove the mystery of it. It is not a magic box; it really is just a bunch of cables, wires and electricity.

➥ **Lesson Activity:** *Show-and-Tell Hardware*

- 🕐 Flexible (20–50 mins)

- Students: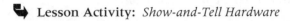

- Preparation: Equipment needs to be gathered; set up before lesson (about 15 mins).

You may wish to set this up in a different room which can be locked, so it can be prepared beforehand.

Gather a range of equipment and place it on a table in a random arrangement. Label each item with a number. This activity allows students to pick up equipment, to see what is inside a computer and not be scared of alien pieces of equipment.

The equipment can include: desktop computer, laptop, floppy disk, CD, DVD, tape, USB memory stick, zip disk, hard disk drive, keyboard, mouse, camera, scanner, microphone, speakers, CRT monitor, LCD monitor, dot matrix printer, inkjet printer, laser printer, network card and any other pieces you can include.

Your school's IT Support should be able to provide some of this equipment and are a fantastic source of ideas and resources for these types of activities. Ask as soon as possible if they can keep broken equipment for you, whether whole computers or single parts. As you will not be using any of this equipment, it does not matter that it is not functional.

If an item cannot be found, such as a dot matrix printer, use a picture of one and ask students to suggest why there is no actual piece of equipment available.

Either use a worksheet to ask about each piece of equipment, or run a 'live quiz' where you ask questions about them (see the companion website for resources). Students could be in pairs or teams depending on the size of the class. As they begin the task you could give them some time to inspect the objects, like at an auction house, before beginning to answer questions.

Questions could start by asking students to identify each part, referring to each by their number, e.g. 'What number is the keyboard?' or 'What is the name of item number 6?'

You could then ask for some facts about the objects: 'Which items contain magnets?', for example, or, 'Which items are peripherals?' or perhaps, 'Which item is referred to as a 3½ inch and can be single- or double-sided?'

You could even include more qualitative questions such as, 'I need to store a large graphic file to take to a meeting with a client – what should I use and why?' or, 'I am printing a high-colour image – what would be best and why?'

As students are mostly writing the numbers of the objects or short names, questions can be answered quite quickly and so the length of this activity is determined by the amount of questions you ask.

It is also interesting and useful for students to see inside a computer, even if they are not planning to become ICT specialists. Seeing inside a computer and understanding that all it is is wires and cables removes some of the mystery and helps build confidence in using them.

It is a useful activity to ask them to draw the inside of a computer, either realistically (possibly teaming up with the Art department) or diagrammatically to show how the CPU and other components join together. Another way of doing this is to use Lego to represent the different parts. This is a very tactile and kinaesthetic activity, and therefore a really good way of getting students with special educational needs (SEN, e.g. autistic students) excited about computers.

This activity is very inclusive as it encourages all students to get involved and enables all of them to achieve and make progress. Students with limited ICT experience can be supported and develop confidence; students whose ICT knowledge is stronger can be challenged. ICT is an excellent subject to promote inclusion, and differentiation is an integral part, often occurring without needing to be forced.

Always be aware of opportunities for inclusion and elements of ICT where the weaker students can be encouraged to demonstrate their progress and higher achievers can really be stretched.

Do not forget those in the middle, of course, and make sure they are supported and pushed as needed. Use praise and enthusiasm to encourage interest, excitement and commitment to the activity and to create an environment where learning takes place naturally.

When you are planning your lessons, always remember the different ways in which students learn, the basic three types being visual, auditory and kinaesthetic. Try to include at least one element for each type in all of your lessons. For example, when doing a demo of some software you can explain it verbally *and* show it on a whiteboard *and* ask the students to follow along with you on their screens – targeting all three major learning styles in one go.

Tactile activities are excellent for students with special needs or learning difficulties. It allows them to explore the ideas through a medium with which they are familiar: touch. Understanding concepts may be challenging, but by being able to see and feel a reality, whether it is an object or something on screen, can enable these students to grasp the ideas in a different way. ICT is an empowering subject and one which is often a positive experience for those who learn in a way that is atypical. Every student learns differently and ICT presents opportunities for allowing access through different approaches.

Lesson Activity: *Under the Bonnet*

- Flexible (30–50 mins)

- Students: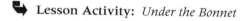

- Preparation: Equipment needs to be gathered; set-up is very quick. Present students with a computer's base unit.

As you will not be using this computer, it could be a broken one. Your IT Support might be able to help you with inoperable equipment. Recycle this unusable equipment by rescuing it from going in the skip and using it in your lessons. Storage can be an issue, but as it is already broken it does not need to be stored safely like normal computer equipment. See if you can locate a partially used cupboard in school, perhaps using the back of another subject's half-filled storage space; maybe it can be put under a desk or in the staff room.

Take students through dismantling the computer step by step, by taking off the lid, looking inside and removing parts such as the hard drive, RAM, etc. For each one describe what it is and discuss what it does. Pass the parts around for students to look at more closely.

> If you do not feel confident in doing this demonstration yourself, perhaps your IT Support could help. Perhaps another member of staff is familiar with taking computers apart, or you could ask a student in an older class who may like building computers at home to do the demonstration.

Extend this activity: If you can gather enough computers, after the demonstration, students can divide into pairs or teams and take apart computers themselves – and then reassemble them correctly.

Extend this activity: As well as taking apart a computer for demonstration, you could also disassemble a laptop for comparison. Another excellent comparison is to show the innards of an Xbox, as it essentially has the same components as a computer but they are arranged differently and have different ratios (e.g. less RAM, more graphic capabilities). An original Xbox is best for this activity – and cheaper! Ask a local games store if they have any broken equipment you could use in your school.

If you only have one lesson to deliver the topic of hardware, you could run these two Lesson Activities side by side, splitting the class into two groups.

- First 30 minutes:
  - ~ group A does *Show-and-Tell Hardware*
  - ~ group B does *Under the Bonnet* with you.
- Second 30 minutes: vice versa.

In this lesson, it would be useful to set a homework exercise to reinforce learning, even something simple such as 'Write 100 words on what you did in each activity and then state five things you learned today which you did not know before.'

Interface

Students will have been using interfaces for as long as they have been using computers, which for many of them will be their entire lives.

22

However, they may not have come across the word 'interface' before or ever really thought about what is involved in an interface.

> 🔑 It is important to not only know how to use something but also to understand what each element is called, so students can use it more effectively. If they are asked to do a task, such as maximize their window, it is important that they know what the request means and how to carry it out.

➡ **Lesson Activity:** *Giant Interface*

- 🕐 Flexible (30–50 mins)
- Students:
- Preparation: Resources to be prepared; no set-up needed. In this activity the students become an interface. You will need:
  ~ single-sided signs for students to hold (large words printed on A4 paper) saying 'Close', 'Mouse', 'Taskbar', 'Toolbar' and 'Icons'
  ~ double-sided signs for students to hold saying 'Maximize/Minimize' and 'Restore Up/Restore Down'
  ~ 4 × adjustable lengths such as bungee ropes or Slinky springs.
  (See this book's companion website for resources).

> 🚩 This task will involve students standing up and moving around. If you do not have room in your classroom, you may choose to move into a larger space such as a gym, foyer or outside.

Ask four students to become the Window and ask them to stand in a square, facing inwards, with the bungee rope or similar between them, round their waists.

Hand out the signs to other students. 'Maximize/Minimize', 'Restore Up/Restore Down' and 'Close' will stand in the 'top right' of the Window and need to work together. 'Toolbar' and 'Icons' will need to work together and stand in the 'top left'. 'Taskbar' stands outside the window to the 'bottom left'. 'Mouse' is free to roam wherever it wants.

The remainder of the students become the User. They choose what will happen and direct the Mouse to perform different actions. When the Mouse 'clicks' on a function, the Window and all those involved need to react appropriately. For example, when the User directs the Mouse to 'click' on 'Minimize', the Window and everyone inside should move to stand beside the Taskbar. 'Maximize/Minimize' needs to remember to turn their card so it is possible to maximize the Window again.

⇨ **Extend this activity**: This activity could also be used to compare standard Windows and Mac interfaces or different versions of Windows operating systems.

Files, folders and saving

Students will generally know how to save files, but very often their areas will become chaotic with nonsensical filenames and a lack of folders, and they will not be able to find the files they need. Further to this, it is useful for them to understand how to recognize different file types, by extension and by icon. I find students are fascinated that each icon has been designed meticulously, that someone has spent hours, sometimes even days or weeks, creating something which they find quite insignificant.

⚷ Explaining icons to students enables them to begin to look at items on the computer differently and this often leads them to ask 'Has everything on the screen been designed?' I ask them to look at their desktop (whether it is Windows or a specific school image) and ask if they have ever thought about this image that they see every day. I then ask them to consider computer games they have played and ask what has been designed – they will often say characters, vehicles, etc., but ask them to consider that each tree, building and cloud in the sky also had to be created, even if they are whizzing past it on a race track. Getting them to consider exactly what goes into software creation leads to them looking at computers in a different way. They realize that software is not just something which happens; it needs to be entirely created.

↳ **Lesson Activity:** *File Types Snap*

- 🕐 Approx. 10 mins

- Students: 👥

- Preparation: Resources to be prepared; no set-up needed.

You will need to create a set of cards for each pair of students with file icons and file extensions, such as .doc, .txt, .xls and .mdb, and the corresponding icons for Word, Notepad, Excel and Access (see this book's companion website for resources). You could also include different types of image files such as .bmp and .jpg where the icons will be the same, whichever program they open with, e.g. Paint, Photoshop – this will depend on the set-up at your school. The icons could be obtained by using screenshots. To make the packs of cards larger, make duplicates of each, so for example each pack has two .doc and two Word icons, always making sure there are pairs and that the activity will work in practice.

When students are in their pairs, each will receive a set of cards. They shuffle them and split them between them evenly. They will then play *Snap*, where they each take turns to place their cards face up on separate piles. If a matching icon and extension are laid down, the first to shout the type of file it is wins all the cards in the piles. If two matching icons or two matching extensions are placed down, the first to shout out the type of file it is wins those two cards only. The winner is the student with all the cards. If the activity is taking longer than the allocated time, you could call for everyone to stop and count up – the student in the pair with the most cards wins.

Email

Email is a vital form of communication and absolutely integral to modern interaction. Most students will be able to send an email; however, you may be surprised how few will fully understand attachments, CC, BCC and other features such as distribution lists.

Whether your students use a program version of email, like Outlook, or a web-based email such as Google Mail, there are standard tools available in all types of email which will be of great use to your students, not just in the future but right now as well.

Activities about email are most useful when taught as early as possible, for example as soon as students join your school and start ICT lessons. This means they will have a good understanding of communicating through email from the beginning and can communicate with each other and with teachers. You may find that a good proportion of your class know these principles already, so they can be taught in short activities, perhaps as starters for your first two or three lessons with them. Used as starters, you will catch them at their most receptive point of the lesson and by keeping the activities short you are not giving them time to get distracted or disruptive.

> After teaching students how to communicate effectively using ICT, you can then use this as your 'official' form of communication in school. Rather than students catching you in the corridor, you can ask them to email you – and each time they do, they are practising an ICT skill. Also, you can ask them to email work to you. This not only saves on printing but also, for interactive files like spreadsheets, it is much easier to assess or help with their work if you can see it in action.

Lesson Activity: *Chinese Whispers*

- 🕐 Approx. 10 mins
- Students:
- Preparation: ⚡

You send an email to a student in the class, with an attachment saying, 'I went to the shops and I bought . . .' and, underneath that, one item added.

That student should open the attachment, add an item to it and then send it on to another student.

> 🚩 Depending on your email system, they may need to save the attachment before sending it on.

To prevent other students getting bored while they wait for their turn, you could send more emails around:

- 'I went on holiday and I packed . . .'
- 'I went to a restaurant and I ate . . .'

- 'I played rugby and I injured my . . .'
- 'I travelled round the world and I saw . . .'

When the messages have been added to by enough people, ask for them to send it on one more time and ask whomever receives the messages to stand up and read out the list. It will probably be amusing and memorable for your students.

Information and the internet

ICT not only covers the operation of a computer but also information and how to work with it effectively. This generally includes how to use search engines effectively, evaluating information for reliability, and can even be using other resources such as the library – a nice opportunity for teaming up with your school librarian who will likely be a fantastic source of information and ideas.

> By teaching students early in their education about how to research effectively, you are not only giving them skills they can use throughout your subject but also in all other subjects as well.

Lesson Activity: *Information Treasure Hunt*

- 🕐 1–2 lessons

- Students: 👥

- Preparation: Resources to be prepared; no set-up needed.

There are four parts to this activity, with the final part being a treasure hunt. You may choose to do all four, in which case the activity will take two 1-hour lessons. However, as with all the activities in this book, you can tailor them to your own students and mix and match.

To make this whole activity more exciting, you may wish to run it as a competition. Students work in their pairs, earning points for each part of the activity. The points can be totalled at the end to find the winners. You could issue bonus points for any moments of inspiration from students or good sportsmanship (e.g. if one team helps another team). You can also deduct points for any bad behaviour or cheating.

> Sometimes prizes for students in schools can be problematic. If your school has a system such as house points or merits, and the students value getting them, then fantastic. It may be that you will need to purchase prizes and perhaps the school will not reimburse you. Prizes for activities such as this should not be expensive. In fact, the cheaper and sillier the prize the better, especially if it gets a laugh. Small, plastic gold medals (like Olympic medals) can often be bought very cheaply (about £1 for ten) and are always popular. Sweets, such as bags of jellies for about 10p, work equally well. Your students, no matter what their age, will not think these are silly or too small – they are tokens that you acknowledge what they have done and appreciate them. If you give them these small items with a big announcement and they then go up to the front and are awarded them, with the rest of the class applauding, it is the moment and recognition which is important to them, rather than what they are receiving.

You might wish to start this activity by asking them what ICT stands for – even though some students have been studying it for years, some will still not know. Once defined, explain how this activity will look at the 'Information' part of the subject.

Part 1 (approx. 15–30 mins): Discussion and demonstration of how to use search engines. They will all have used search engines before and the aim of this is to show them how to use them better. This could include: what search engines are available, using capitals, quotes and keywords, using operators and clever things to do in Google such as define, weather and conversions. Following this, reinforce the learning by asking them to complete a worksheet where they are asked to find answers to questions – which they can only do by looking them up online, such as, 'If you type in the name of your school into Google and Ask, how many hits do you get?' or, 'How would you search in Google to find out what 'Dendrophobia' means – and what does it mean?' (see this book's companion website for resources). When marking these answers, bear in mind that the internet is a living and breathing organism, and their results may vary – such as the number of hits produced by a certain search – but they should be roughly the same.

Part 2 (approx. 15–30 mins): Finding and using information. Discuss where they could get information other than the internet, such as books, newspapers and people. Talk about how they might use their school library, or local library, and ask whether they do use these fantastic resources. This could be followed by a conversation about copyright and plagiarism. When discussing plagiarism, I always remind them that serious cases can end in expulsion from the school and students are always surprised when I tell them that both the copier and the 'copyee' will be punished, as how can we prove who created the work first? A real story of copyright in the law is always useful to demonstrate that people do take copyright very seriously. If there are no recent stories, you may wish to use the case of J. K. Rowling and Steven Vander Ark, as all students should be aware of the Harry Potter books. Part 2 can also be followed by a worksheet where the learning is reinforced and more points can be accumulated (see this book's companion website for resources).

Part 3 (approx. 10–15 mins): Can we trust it? Discuss the validity and reliability of information on the internet. Give your students some questions they can ask about information to see how reliable it is, e.g. Who wrote it? Are they biased? Is it up to date? Is it based on facts, or just an opinion? A great debate at this point can be one about Wikipedia – some of your students may not know it is written by the public and may think it is entirely trustworthy. The worksheet to follow Part 3 could be showing screenshots of websites and asking students to say whether they are reliable or unreliable and why. The screenshots could be of a news story on the BBC website; a news story on a fake news site such as *The Onion*; and a page from Wikipedia.

Part 4 (approx. 20–45 mins): Information Treasure Hunt. Now your students have an understanding of information and how to find it, they are ready to do the Information Treasure Hunt. If possible, have a section where they must use a search engine and the techniques you have covered, and a section using your school library where they must physically go there and answer questions. If you use the library, you need to make sure you ask questions which cannot be found on a search engine. For example, you may wish to ask questions about some of the posters and displays on the walls, or the locations of certain books, which dictionaries are available or the Dewey decimal numbers of certain books. You may wish to set a time limit for the section to add an extra challenge and also to attempt to find a winning pair if the scores from the previous parts are quite similar.

> ☰— It would be overkill to run both of these researching activities together; however, it might be more useful to have one near the beginning of the academic year and the other just before or after Easter. It will provide a refresher on researching and, for year groups who are working on coursework, it will be well placed to remind them of these important techniques.

Lesson Activity: *The Body in the Library (as suggested by Sandra Hall, Librarian)*

- 🕐 1 lesson
- Students: 👥
- Preparation: Needs preparation and time to set up before lesson.

> ⚐ This activity needs to take place entirely in the school library, so make sure you book the library. You may find that your school librarian is enthusiastic to help you as you are encouraging your students to use the library more.

The aim of this activity is to use researching techniques to find out 'whodunit'. I would advise keeping this activity very light and bringing humour into it. For example, you may wish to describe the nature of the murder and make it quite outlandish or improbable, or just have the victim injured. 'The Librarian was replacing a book on the top shelf when someone ran in and pushed her off the ladder and she fell and broke her leg', or, 'Polly the school cat ate the lunch that had been prepared for the ICT teacher and it was poisoned!' Alternatively, they may also have to work out 'whatdunit', like in the board game *Cluedo*.

In preparing the resources for this activity, it will depend on your own school's library as to how you will do it and what you will use. You may wish to organize it so that each clue will lead to the discovery of another clue and so forth. Alternatively, you may give them all the clues at once, which will result in working out who the murderer was. You may also wish to give them a sheet of suspects: these could be fictional people or teachers in the school – although make sure you get those teachers' agreement before including them!

Clues could include:

- The age of the murderer is between Library and Information Sciences and Italian Encyclopaedias (answer: 020–035).
- The initials of the person who wrote 1984 are somewhere in the name of the murderer (answer: G. O.).
- The next clue is a book in which a sarcastic feathered creature is done away with, written by a woman with the initials H. L. (answer: *To Kill a Mockingbird* by Harper Lee).

Your clues will depend on who your murderer and suspects are and what resources you have in your library.

If you also have computers in your library, or a computer room nearby, you could include some clues which they would need to look up on the computer. You could also plant a clue on the school website or inside your VLE.

Before the lesson, you may wish to bring the activity to life by marking out a 'chalk outline' using masking tape on the library floor, or more simply an X for the spot where it happened.

Health and safety

Health and safety is a vital part of ICT and something which should always be remembered when you are responsible for an ICT room. They used to be called computer labs; even though the name has changed, you should still approach it as you would a science lab from a health and safety perspective.

Similarly students should have an appreciation of health and safety when using ICT so they not only use the room correctly, but also protect themselves from permanent injuries.

o— Whenever you see students contravening health and safety advice, whether in a lesson, using a computer in their free time or using a laptop elsewhere in school, always remind them of the correct usage. You don't need to harp on about legislation, but you could remind them that you are only asking them to change their actions in order to protect them from injury and permanent damage. This includes asking them to sit up if they are slouching, making sure lights are on when they are using computer screens, and eating or drinking near equipment. Also,

as a good ICT role model, make sure you are not caught slouching at your computer or trailing your wires dangerously across
the floor!

➥ Lesson Activity: *Infomercials*

- 🕐 Minimum 1 lesson (continue longer if desired)
- Students: 👥
- Preparation: ⚡

This activity would follow a discussion on health and safety rules in ICT
and you may wish to have students get into groups and plan their idea
in the lesson prior to this one, so they have maximum time filming and
editing. Their aim is to create an infomercial in their groups about one
of the health and safety risks in an ICT room. They should aim for just a
few minutes in length.

> 🚩 They will want to re-create the dangerous situations, so
> please make sure you tell them to keep themselves safe
> during this activity. For example, they could use empty water
> bottles, rather than actually bringing water into the ICT room.
> Warn that any dangerous behaviour will have them disqualified
> from the activity.

Allocate each group a risk, e.g. no eating, no drinking, trailing wires, and
set a strict deadline. They will need a device on which to record their
infomercial (see this book's companion website for advice on equipment)
and will need to record and edit their short movies in the set time.

> 🔑 When setting deadlines for creative, fun activities such as
> this one, you need to take into account that they will need
> more time. Try setting your deadline 5 or 10 minutes before the
> actual deadline, then you can look magnanimous when you give
> them that extra time. Since you have given them extra time, you

can then tell them they have to fulfil their end of the bargain and make sure they do not run over again. These types of activities easily run over time and you need to keep hold of the reins very tightly, without making it look like you are. Careful planning, understanding the equipment you are using, and an ability to say a final 'Stop!' are crucial to staying within the time restraints of your lesson. However, if you know your students will enjoy this, you may choose to put this lesson before a break or lunchtime or warn the following teacher they may be late. Perhaps you can let your students out early next week for the next teacher to regain their time with them.

At the end of the lesson, or possibly at the beginning of the next, have a showcase of the films made. If you show them in the following lesson, you could watch them first and have an Oscars-type ceremony and announce the winners in each category, e.g. Best Message, Best Film Work, Best Editing or more humorous categories such as Best Use of a Teacher, Most Dodgy Camera Angles. You will know your students and their sense of humour and what they will enjoy.

➡ **Extend this activity:** You could expand your showcase to include students from other classes, as well as the class who filmed them. If you have several classes doing this activity at one time, you could organize the showcase for a lunchtime and book a large space in which to show the films.

➡ **Extend this activity:** If the films are very good, you could include them on your school's VLE or even their website. If some have good ideas, you could set them a task of re-filming their infomercial in their lunchtimes for a week, saying it will have the honour of it being shown to the rest of the school and the public (including their parents/guardians) as their reward.

Viruses

Viruses are a useful topic to introduce early on to students. Not only is it a part of the syllabus, but it can help protect them when using computers in school and at home. There are two key things they need to know: how to avoid getting a virus and what to do if they get one. Methods for preventing viruses include not accessing unreliable, 'dodgy' websites and not opening emails from senders they do not know, especially if they have attachments. Understanding the importance of anti-virus software and keeping it up to date are also crucial.

> ⚷ To help students understand this topic, which can seem quite abstract to them, an interesting parallel to draw is with human or animal infections. Ask them to consider how viruses such as influenza are passed from person to person. Examine how some viruses are airborne and spread quickly from person to person and how some might be more difficult to transmit. Each virus does something different, and although some can be quite similar (e.g. many produce the symptoms of a cold) they will all be fundamentally different. You could also use mad cow disease as an example, discussing how it was spread and how it was dealt with.

> ⚷ A terminology issue often arises at this point over the difference between a virus (a program to steal or destroy data) and a bug (an error in a software's programming which produces unexpected results).

Once students understand that viruses are not naturally occurring, that someone has to make and spread them, they are usually baffled as to why someone would want to spend their time doing that. There are two main reasons:

- Some viruses are specifically designed to cause chaos, attempting to bring down the world's computer systems, such as the ILOVEYOU virus which spreads through Microsoft Outlook and not only replicates itself to everyone in a user's contact list, but will also delete files such as JPEGs and MP3s from their computer. At its peak it reportedly spread to 45 million machines in one day.
- Other viruses are more dastardly, trying to steal data such as a contacts list, change data such as exam grades or bank accounts or steal money stored electronically. As computer security has increased, identity theft has increasingly become the object of viruses which target account and personal details and return them to the virus' creator.

Lesson Activity: *Infection!*

- 🕐 Approx. 15 mins
- Students: 👥
- Preparation: Cards to be prepared; no set-up needed in the lesson.

The aim of this activity is to show how files become infected and learn about different types of viruses.

In preparation for this activity you will need to create a set of cards (or download them from this book's companion website):

- 1 virus card:

'VIRUS – When it is your turn, shout "Virus" and tap the shoulders of the people either side of you, who are then infected. Continue tapping people on the shoulder and infecting them, until ANTI-VIRUS arrives.'

- 1 trojan card:

'TROJAN – When it is your turn, pretend to be a document. When it is your next turn, pretend to be an image file. Keep changing until you are spotted and ANTI-VIRUS arrives.'

- 1 worm card:

'WORM – When it is your turn, you are infected and pass your card on to someone else. Do this as quickly as possible.

IF YOU RECEIVE THIS CARD FROM ANOTHER PERSON you have been infected – pass it on to someone else. Do this as quickly as possible.'

- Several cards displaying a file type, e.g. 'WORD DOCUMENT – when it is your turn, state clearly what type of file you are.' Make sure you have enough of these for everyone else in your class.

In the lesson, ask your students to sit in a circle. Explain that they are all going to be files but if they become infected they are 'out'. Shuffle the cards and deal one to each person (if you have extra cards or any students missing, make sure you include the three virus cards without making it obvious). When they receive their cards, make sure they keep them secret and read the instructions on them carefully and silently.

You will also need to sit in the circle as you are ANTI-VIRUS, but do not reveal that until you need to spring into action. Wait for them to say that they need anti-virus software to sort out their problems.

Go round the circle and ask each student to say what type of file they are, unless they are a type of virus, in which case they act out what is on their card. As ANTI-VIRUS, only act if the class discover a virus and say that they need anti-virus to remove it. You can do so by tapping the accused student on the shoulder.

At the end of the activity, analyse who is infected and who is uninfected. This could spark a discussion on how viruses spread, what is good practice to avoid viruses and how to eradicate them.

⇨ **Expand this activity:** You could have more than one of each type of virus. You could also be an out-of-date ANTI-VIRUS that has not been updated, meaning that you will not have any effect on some of the viruses until you have been updated. Perhaps one of the students could be your update or, with some clever timing and a willing volunteer (such as an IT technician), you could have someone turn up at your classroom with the 'update' during this activity and then you can eradicate all the viruses before they damage more files. If the activity is moving quickly, once you have been updated you may wish to run a 'scan' of the whole computer system.

Legislation in ICT

Legislation – a word that strikes fear at the heart of both teachers and students. Teachers dread it because the concepts involved are often quite abstract – it is not a practical area that involves learning computer skills and is generally the area which students will find hardest to learn. Students dislike it because they think it is boring: lots of facts and figures and nothing really relevant to them. This is your opportunity to prove them, and your fellow teachers, wrong. This is your opportunity to stand out. This is a great topic for interviews or inspections – any teacher can pull off an interesting lesson on building web pages; it is much rarer to find a lesson on legislation which has students focused, attentive and learning throughout.

Students often ask, 'Why do we have to learn about legislation? What relevance does it have to us?' You can answer: 'Everything. Every time you use a computer, these laws affect you.' If they (or their parents/guardians, older siblings, etc.) buy items online, then the Data Protection Act 2003 (DPA) comes into force and keeps their data safe. The same applies to when they are registering with web email or social networking sites. Speaking of email and social networking, the Computer Misuse Act 1990 (CMA) is there to protect them from their profiles being hacked into and from infection by viruses. The Obscene Publications Act 1959 is to prevent them being exposed to unsavoury material online, such as pornography or violence. Laws on copyright (e.g. the Copyright, Designs and Patents Act 1988) are there to protect anything they might create in the future, whether it be a website for their company, a piece of music or whatever their aspirations might lead them to. It is also worth reminding them that in a court of law, ignorance is not an excuse. When they ask why you have said that, you can joke that if they are arrested for illegally downloading music or software, at least they'll know under which Act they've been arrested!

⮩ Lesson Activity: *How Safe is Your Data?*

- 🕐 Approx. 30 mins

- Students: 👥

- Preparation: ⚡

The aim of this activity is to get students thinking about personal information and what could happen if they pass it to other people. By seeing it in action, it will help them understand the realities of the DPA and why it is so important.

Ask for four volunteers: they will be 'services'. Stand one in each corner of the room and name them: 'Hospital', 'Bank', 'University', 'Website'. Each needs a piece of paper and a pen for recording the data they obtain. (A clipboard might also be useful and, if you really want to get them into character, use props such as a hat for 'Bank', toy stethoscope for 'Hospital', etc.)

Divide the remainder of the students into three teams. They will each need a pen and paper (and a clipboard if you have them). They will each be a person and their aim is to get access to the four services in the room. However, they will need to give some data in order to achieve that. First, they need to decide on the kind of person they are and write down as much information about them as they think would be adequate and relevant (terms used by the DPA). (If your services are in character, you could enhance the teams' experience by giving them dolls/figures to inspire their 'people'.)

While the teams are working out (and likely arguing over) their person, you quickly speak to each of your 'services', because they are not going to be quite as lawful as you would expect.

- **Hospital** will write down all of the information but as though the person was a baby (breaking the principle of 'up to date').

- **University** will try to take as much information as possible (breaking the principle of 'adequate, relevant and not excessive').
- **Bank** will try to take as much information as possible (as above) and then, when they can, sneak up to the whiteboard and write on as much as they can, trying not to be noticed (breaking the principle of 'secure').
- **Website** will write down all of the information incorrectly (breaking the principle of 'accurate').

When your services and teams are all ready, explain that due to a set of unusual circumstances their 'people' have broken their legs, need a bank loan, have decided to apply for a degree and want to buy some clothes from a website all at the same time! Each team needs to take their 'person' to each service and register with them. Advise them that only one team can speak to a service at a time.

Allow the activity to run. It might get noisy and a little chaotic, but as long as they are all on task that is fine.

Once the 'people' have visited all four services, ask the services to come to the front and everyone else to sit down. Ask each service to read out the information they obtained from the 'people'. There are two ways this might go: the 'people' handed over all their information, in which case ask them to guess which principle of the DPA has been broken. On the other hand, the 'people' may have been more cautious and savvy, in which case ask them why they didn't want to hand over their information and then ask the service to explain their instructions before discussing the principles of the DPA.

This should lead smoothly into a whole-class discussion about all the principles of the DPA and how it operates, referring to the activity as examples (e.g. 'What if the university had links with an educational programme in a remote part of the world and passed them your details because they thought you might be interested in it?' Consider the DPA's principle on not passing information to countries with a lower level of data protection).

➡ **Extend this activity**: Ask your students to think about their own data. Do they get junk mail or spam? How did that happen? Do they shred their mail? Did they know people will steal bins to get data? Have they registered on websites that might be a little dodgy? Have they shared their passwords with anyone or written them down? There are lots of branches this topic can lead to – if this discussion becomes quite wide and your students are enthusiastic, perhaps they could draw a mind map on the topic for homework.

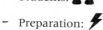

Lesson Activity: *Ethical Dilemmas*

- 🕐 1 lesson
- Students: 👥
- Preparation: ⚡

The aim of this activity is to discuss issues relating to various legislation and most situations will cross over into others which is inevitable with ICT issues. Both the discussion of the issue and the discussion about which laws may apply will be interesting.

Examples of the ethical dilemmas could include:

- Your friend is interested in hacking and has found a weakness in the website of a controversial group, with whose views you disagree. He thinks that he would be able to get into the website, make changes and then remove any trace of him being there. What do you advise him to do?
- You are the administrator on a forum where you invite people to come to discuss issues. Its aim was to promote free speech and generate genuine discussion. However, you now have a user who is being rude and offensive, posting messages which are upsetting you and other users. You could ban them, but wouldn't that go against the point of your website? What would you do?
- A friend of yours enjoys making small programs in her spare time. She shows you her latest one and you realize it is a virus that will send her people's credit card details which she can then use to buy anything online. She says she's just exploiting a weakness that shouldn't have been left open and that if she doesn't use it, someone else will. She offers to cut you in if you don't say anything. What do you do?
- A friend of yours offers to sell you a recently released film which you have been waiting to see. You hand over the money, but it is only when you get it home that you realize it is an illegal copy. You know illegal downloading and copying of films is wrong, but you have now purchased a pirated copy. What do you do?
- You are messing around on the school computers one day and accidently discover you have access to the system where your school records are kept. You could go in and change your current predicated grade, or you could look up the phone number of that person you quite fancy. You realize that this has to be some sort of network error and that the technicians could be aware of it and will correct it soon.

You have to make a quick decision. What do you do? (More dilemmas available on this book's companion website.)

If there are topical ethical ICT issues in the news at the time of delivery of this Lesson Activity, include them, because they might provoke interesting and involved discussions.

Divide your class into five groups and arrange them so each team is sat together, away from the others.

> As computers are not needed for this activity, you may wish to move this lesson to a standard classroom, where you could arrange the desks in five blocks, one for each team. If you do so, when you put the class into groups, ask them to move the tables and chairs. This will make it a much quicker process – remember to ask them to put them back at the end of the lesson.

Put pens and paper on each table. Give each team an ethical dilemma.

> You could distribute the ethical dilemmas by writing them on the board, numbering them, then giving each table a number; or writing them on slips of paper and handing them out – this could be done while your students are rearranging the desks. If you have time for preparation, making cards with the dilemmas on and laminating them means you will be able to use them with other classes and keep them for each year when you teach this lesson (pre-prepared materials are available on this book's companion website, meaning less preparation time is needed for the lesson).

Give each team 8 minutes to discuss their dilemma and make notes (brief bullet points) on the key factors and any decisions they make about it.

Once those 8 minutes are up, ask each team to turn their notes face down on the table, leave the notes, pens and dilemma where they are, and move clockwise to the next table. Here, they discuss the new dilemma, then turn over the previous team's notes and add their own thoughts and comments, perhaps marking whether they agree or disagree with the previous team.

As each team tackles the different dilemmas, you could visit each table and throw in extra suggestions or factors they should take into account, or give them a wider perspective than they may have.

The activity is complete once all five teams have deliberated over each dilemma. Move each team back to their original table and allow them to read all of the notes which have been added to theirs throughout the lesson. Depending on time, ask each team to provide a spokesperson to feed back on the key points of each issue.

⇨ **Extend this activity**: For each issue, ask which law is primarily involved, and which could also come into play. Perhaps also ask them to suggest what punishments would be appropriate (if applicable).

⇨ **Extend this activity**: Ask them to prepare a presentation in their teams to be delivered in the following ICT lesson. They must show all sides of the issue objectively and include some research, then come to a conclusion on their team's majority opinion on the issue.

Collaborative tools

Web 2.0 is the term used to describe a huge range of interactive and collaborative tools which are available. In education they are extremely useful, and are also being used throughout business. Therefore it is important for students to understand how to use them effectively so they can take part in growing online culture. Although they may already be savvy at using collaborative tools such as social networking, it is useful for them to know a greater range of what is available.

Your school is likely to have a VLE, so your students will be aware of a collaborative tool – but have they used it properly? It is often assumed that 'someone else' will teach them how to use it, as is the case with study skills, how to research, etc. Topics such as this do need to be taught because although some students will find it easy to play with the VLE and work it out for themselves, the majority will need to be shown how to use it. The best way to go about this is to be proactive and take it onboard as part of the ICT curriculum, as it is the most logical place for it (or as part of the tutorial programme). Make sure if you are providing lessons on your VLE that it is done early when the students join the school so that it becomes part of everyday life at school, rather than something extra they need to deal with. Also make sure your senior management are aware you are running these lessons, so they are not duplicated elsewhere.

Collaborative tools other than your VLE are widely available and you should endeavour to show your students as many as possible. It may be that you demonstrate a tool at the end of each lesson and set homework for them to use it. For example, at the end of a lesson you could demonstrate a shared bookmarking site and set students the task of creating a profile on the site and bookmarking ten pages using this tool. Alternatively, you may wish to use these tools as part of an extra-curricular project (see page 105), such as creating a blog about ICT lessons or podcasts about school life (to be seen within the school, or perhaps also shown on the school website).

The history of ICT

It is useful for students to have an understanding of the history of ICT. They can gain an appreciation of how things have developed, of moments of genius, of key figures in ICT's history and of the speed at which we moved from computers which filled a room to ones no bigger than your palm and which do vastly more tasks in the blink of an eye.

➥ Lesson Activity: *What Did We Do Before?*

- 🕐 1 lesson

- Students: 👥

- Preparation: ⚡

The aim of this lesson is for students to consider the impact of ICT on society and the individual.

Ask students to get into pairs. Give them an ICT invention from the years the class were born (e.g. 1997 and 1998) – don't tell them that this is the connection between these things. For suggestions of inventions, see this book's companion website.

Give the pairs 5–10 minutes to discuss the invention in their pairs:

- What is it used for?
- Who uses it?

(If they are unsure what it is, they can quickly look it up online.)

Ask each group to feed back their thoughts to the class. Now do the big reveal (with gusto!) – all of these inventions were created/released in the years that they were born.

Set them a task to makes notes on the following questions about their invention, using the internet for research:

- What is the purpose of the invention?
- What need did the invention fulfil? (Why was it invented?)
- Who invented it?
- What was used before that invention was available? (If applicable, consider what was used before computers.)
- How did it change the life of the individual?
- How did it change society?

Once they have their research, ask them to create a poster/newsletter/presentation about their invention.

⇨ **Expand this activity:** Use this activity to start a discussion on the impact of ICT on the individual and society. Does everyone have equal access in the UK or across the world? How will ICT change in the future?

⇨ **Expand this activity:** Repeat this activity but with some more established technology – for example the personal computer, the games console, the mobile phone – and ask them to really think about what life was like before we had this technology.

Skills-based ICT

In ICT, there are two main schools of thought on delivery of the standard content of the subject. Skills-based ICT teaches students to use certain pieces of software, developing particular skills so that when they are asked to carry out those tasks they are fully able to do so. These will always include the most common tasks needed, such as creating formulae in spreadsheets. Problem-solving ICT (discussed further in the next section) is more about presenting students with problems and asking them to decide how to approach and solve them. Both approaches are equally valid and choosing between them can depend on the types of students being taught, their previous knowledge, their interest in the subject and many other factors. Exam boards and curriculum advisers are split over which approach is best and it is likely to be one of the eternal debates of ICT, therefore as a good teacher of ICT you need to be aware of both approaches and be able to deliver whatever is required or desired.

It is possible to use a combination of the two approaches, getting the best of both worlds, by beginning with skills-based to give them a solid grounding in using common software such as word processing and spreadsheets, then moving on to more problem-based topics so they can use the skills they have developed to tackle the situations with which they are presented. This could be split by year group, for instance younger years first learn skills, then progress in problem-solving in older years. Alternatively, this split could be made within each topic. For example, a topic could start by being about spreadsheets and learning the particular skills needed, then move into an independent project which challenges them with a puzzle which they need to solve, such as, 'Your friend has decided to start his own business and has asked you to help him with the finances. He will provide you with his figures and you must produce clear information for him to use to develop his business.' In this sort of approach, the student must look back at the skills they have learned, decide which are applicable and use them correctly. It does not state which formulae, functions and so on need to be used at which points. You may wish to give more guidance on the sort of results they should produce, perhaps saying their friend needs the data presented in a chart, but they must decide what is useful and appropriate.

Be careful with the word 'appropriate'. Remember that as adults we understand how a document may be appropriate for a business, but young people who have no experience of business have no frame of reference to understand what you are asking them to do. Try showing them examples of what is appropriate and, importantly, what is not. Often we can learn more by seeing bad examples rather than good. Highlight key elements they should include and ones which they should avoid.

The following sections contain practical advice, lesson ideas and strategies which you can use to teach skills-based ICT. They will cover the topics of word processing, presentation, spreadsheets and databases, as these are the most common skills to be taught and those which would be useful for all people going into business. For the section on multimedia, see page 63. The intention here is to provide advice and suggestions for lessons for use with any software, as there are similar integral elements in each one, rather than to teach you subject knowledge.

first topic to cover

Word processing

Word processing programs are the programs your students will go on to use the most, as they are used everywhere in education and employment. They are often overlooked because is it assumed that students will already be proficient in these basic skills. Typing up a piece of coursework is still using ICT, no matter how basic and straightforward it may seem. Most of your students will arrive in your school with the ability to word process, therefore teaching them this topic may seem easy; but they will have picked up bad habits along the way. The one that I see the most, and is often the hardest to break, is using the space bar to move a title to the centre of the page, rather than using the centre alignment tool.

As they will know how to word process already, you may be tempted to save time and just give them a task, and hope to correct usage of the software as you go around. However, you can't be everywhere at once to correct each time a student bashes the space bar instead of using the alignment tools. It is useful to approach word processing like other topics and make sure they have a good understanding before beginning their own tasks. You may worry that they will find it boring to talk about a piece of software they have likely been using for several years; however, it is much easier to highlight key areas to the whole group at the beginning than try to firefight for the rest of the task, and probably every time they have to word process after that. The other teachers in your school will presume that the students have learned how to word process effectively in ICT.

Rather than approaching it as being something they know already and might find boring, you could say at the beginning that they are already experts in one of the most important areas of ICT, and this introduction is their chance to show you exactly what they know. You might even wish to put them into teams, and give prizes to the team who give the most right answers.

Your introduction could include fonts, formatting (bold, italics, etc.), bullets and numbering, inserting images, alignment and other key areas. You could also show the toolbars in your word processing program and see how many of the icons they can name.

Lesson activities to teach word processing are a bit redundant as the best way to learn the software is to get on and actually use it. Although inventing a topic to tackle using word processing can be tricky, it is also a fantastic opportunity. This is especially important if this is the first ICT project your class undertakes. This is where you can sell your subject to them and get them to love ICT; it's an opportunity to show them it is a truly exciting subject.

⚷   When it comes to setting tasks and projects ICT has the problem of there needing to be some kind of purpose or topic. If you want to do a project using word processing, or a spreadsheet, or set a task so they choose which software they are using, you will still need to invent a brief for them to fulfil. This creates the problem of coming up with something new for every task, but is an opportunity to get your students excited and interested in what they are doing. The principle of 'learning through play' should not be limited to primary education; it can be extended to secondary, further education, higher education and even to teaching adults. Learning is a much more enjoyable process when it is fun, and if you can select a topic which engages your students they will focus on the topic and the learning will just happen, seemingly almost as a by-product, but it will happen. Use this opportunity to set a task that is fascinating, that will get all of your students on board and will allow learning to be enjoyable and not forced.

A word processing project gives you a great opportunity to link up with other subjects, so rather than having to invent a topic by yourself, you can have something more real. Also, using cross-curriculum link-ups, both subjects should benefit – you get a more credible topic; the other subject either has their teaching reinforced or they gain more time (your lesson(s)), to deliver their curriculum. For example, your English department had planned to teach their Year 7 students how to write letters – if they link up with ICT, they can deliver the formatting of a letter, and you can show them how to format it with word processing software. This might only take two lessons, one from each subject, rather than more lessons and possible duplication. Alternatively, History may have been teaching Year 8 about Henry VIII – if they link up with ICT, the students could learn about Henry VIII in their History lessons and in ICT draw family trees, write personal ads for Henry when he is looking for each of his new wives or create diaries written by each of his wives. There is a lot of scope for link-ups in this area. Teachers of other subjects are bound to have exciting ideas and will often be happy that you have shown an interest in their subject and want to link up. Approach them by explaining how it will benefit them and the students you both teach. They are bound to be brimming with ideas.

There is also a lot of scope for competitions and wall displays in this area. Adding an element of competition will see most young people up their game, especially if it is something they would like to win and is sold to them well. However, when thinking about prizes, don't just consider items which can be bought – think more about recognition. The prizes could include the best pieces of work being:

- put on a wall display in the corridor or in a central place in school (such as a foyer or eating area) which a lot of students and staff use
- included in a school magazine
- displayed on the school website or VLE
- used for a school event (such as invitations).

Young people really respond when you give them praise in class. With this praise coming from a teacher and in front of a group of their peers, it can make a genuine difference to attitude and effort. If the praise is amplified so that it comes from more members of staff, the head, the whole year group or all students in the school, perhaps even parents and the general public, the attitude and effort usually increases. Even if students say that recognition isn't important to them, or there is bravado suggesting that sort of thing just isn't 'cool' enough, underneath all young people want to be recognized for doing something well.

A proportion of your students may be struggling in all other subjects, and perhaps the more academic, written subjects are proving impossible for them. ICT is often a place where these students can shine. As it is a more vocational and practical subject, it can be an alternative and a 'safe' place for them to learn, somewhere where they are able to achieve, where they can be interested, and where they do not constantly struggle or fail. For these students, getting recognition in ICT that extends outside the classroom is an opportunity to show their worth, to demonstrate to their other teachers that they are able to do well in a subject.

Lesson Activity: *Topics for Word Processing*

Some possible tasks for word processing you may like to consider using include:

- writing a letter – to their friend, parents, a teacher, a famous person (alive or from history) or someone overseas
- creating a CV – for themselves, a character from a book or film or someone famous
- crafting a poem or song lyrics
- composing a short story
- designing invitations – for a party or school event
- writing a journal, diary or blog – about themselves, a character or someone famous
- conceiving a menu or recipe
- designing a programme for a school play or sport event
- devising a quiz or questionnaire – to give to other students or classes
- creating a family tree – about their family (could link with PSHE/ Citizenship) or someone from history.

Desktop publishing

Desktop publishing (DTP) is very similar to word processing in that students will enter your school having very likely used this software and other teachers will assume they can do it. You may find other subjects setting tasks for students to create newsletters, leaflets and brochures, assuming that they will be able to do it. It is therefore useful for your students to know early on how to create these things. Depending on which software you use, DTP software is often very similar to word processing software and within the same suite of programs, therefore you will not generally need to teach any new skills, merely point out the few differences and let them get on and use it.

Again there are some fantastic opportunities for cross-curriculum link-ups in this area, for example creating newspapers from times in History or newsletters written in French or German, or even creating products for the whole school, such as a school magazine.

↳ Lesson Activity: *Topics for Desktop Publishing*

Some possible tasks for desktop publishing you may like to consider using include:

- creating a newsletter, newspaper or magazine
- creating a poster (possibly for a campaign, e.g. 'Keep Your ICT Room Tidy' or 'Help Your School Go Green')
- creating a brochure (perhaps for a holiday destination)
- creating a catalogue or stock list (perhaps for your school's sports equipment).

Presentations

When beginning to teach your students about presentations, you will get two reactions. Some of your students will relish the idea of standing up, speaking to an audience (whether that be the class or a larger group of people) and will feel confident and look forward to the final task which inevitably will be delivering their presentation. Others will think this project is the worst thing in the world. It is their worst nightmare to stand up in front of people and speak. They will try to do anything to avoid it. However, being able to deliver a presentation is a very important skill and one better learned now (with mistakes made and the process of overcoming fear begun) rather than having to give their first presentation at university or for employers. They will try to get out of it: mysteriously lose their voice, pull a sickie, claim there has been a bereavement in the family – anything and everything to try to avoid it. You should manage this situation carefully. If you do not approach it in an appropriate way, there is a risk you could make the situation worse. Imagine these scenarios:

You announce that your students will be delivering presentations to the class in two lessons' time. Most are jubilant, but you spot one boy who looks very unhappy at the prospect and you know him to be quite shy normally.

Scenario 1: You ignore this reaction. Everyone has to do it and it will be good for him in the future, so he just needs to accept it and to get on with it.

Scenario 2: As the class starts working on a task, he puts his hand up. You stand beside him as he asks, 'Do I really have to do it?' You reply, 'Yes, everyone has to do it. Now get on with preparing your presentation otherwise you'll be stood up there with nothing to say!'

Scenario 3: As the class starts working on a task, he puts his hand up. You stand beside him as he asks, 'Do I really have to do it?' You kneel beside his chair to be the same height as him and smile, saying, 'I know you find this difficult, but it is a really good skill for you to learn for the future. And do you know what – I believe in you and I know that you can do this well.'

I have often been surprised by students who are quiet or introverted, or have SEN issues which generally hamper their progress, who suddenly come alive when they give presentations. If you show that you believe in them, if you understand their worries and have faith in them, this goes a long way to building their confidence so that they can stand in front of people and deliver their presentation. Advising them to practise also helps, as with practice they will know what to say, rather than stumbling over their words and letting the fear of being in front of people take over.

○━ I find that the most powerful tool in teaching is not praise or exciting activities, although these are very important – the one element that can cause huge improvements in the effort level of your students, that can move a student's grade from the bottom to the top, that can transform a volatile classroom into one of harmony, is believing in your students, is showing that you believe in them. It sounds so simple, and yet it truly can be the one thing that revolutionizes your teaching. Not only should you believe in your students, but you also need to convey it.

When you meet them for the first time, tell them how well you know they are going to achieve, how you believe they are all capable of the highest grades. At the beginning of lessons, especially ones you know will be tricky, reassure them that you are confident they will be able to grasp the concepts and do well. On an individual basis, when you see their confidence in themselves is wavering, or they think they cannot do it, remind them that you believe they *can* do it.

By showing them that you believe in your students you will instil a confidence in them, one that they may never have experienced before. For those students who have always struggled or always misbehaved, perhaps no one has ever believed in them before. Perhaps they are always being told – by teachers, by parents, by peers – that they are worthless, that they will never amount to anything, that they will never make anything of themselves. If you show them that you believe in them, they will respond.

I have seen students' grades change from U to A*, from Fail to Distinction, mostly just through believing in them and having high expectations. If a student reaches a C or a B and wants to stop, don't let them – if there is time to go for the A or A*, keep pushing and believing. Sometimes they will fall short of the high level you have set for them, but at least they have tried their best and that is something of which they can be proud. Never promise them that they will get the very highest grades, but always urge them on to strive for them.

Presentations can be delivered not only in class but also you could have them performed on a larger scale. You could ask another class of older or younger students to join yours to create a larger audience; perhaps you could ask another teacher to watch the presentations and give feedback. You could even put students into groups and set the preparation of the presentations for homework only – then each week in assembly or similar school gathering each group delivers their presentation to the whole school and all the teachers, the topics being interesting to everyone.

↳ Lesson Activity: *Topics for Presentations*

When setting topics for presentations, try to make them interesting not only for your students to prepare and deliver, but also for your audience to listen to. There is nothing more boring than hearing 20 or 30 presentations on the same thing! If you want an attentive audience, make sure the presentation topics are interesting and varied.

Some possible ideas for presentations you may like to consider using include:

- allow students to choose their own topic (something that is interesting to them)
- link up with other subjects and set the topic based on their current learning in those subjects
- on this day in history, or the day the student was born
- pair up students, ask them to think of a topic, then swap topics with their partner, e.g. Beth chooses 'cats', Stephanie chooses 'football' and therefore Beth does a presentation on football and Stephanie on cats (it's best to only reveal the swap after they have chosen their topics, although there will always be some conspiring to pick things that they are both interested in)
- my dream holiday
- what I would do if I won the lottery
- topics which need research – obscure things which they will not have studied in other subjects and will likely know nothing about, e.g. steam trains, needlework, etc.

- 25 uses for . . . and give each student a random object such as a paperclip, tennis ball, cardboard box, etc.
- famous people, such as Winston Churchill, Charles Dickens, Marie Curie, Nelson Mandela, Joan of Arc, etc.

⚑ *How to Allocate Topics for Presentations*

Rather than just telling your students the topics for their presentations, you could make it more interesting by using one of the following methods. It will add excitement to the process which otherwise could be a bit staid. These methods will also add an element of randomness and free choice, meaning the student cannot complain about their topic because they chose it.

- Topics chosen out of a hat (the funnier the hat the better).
- Topics are all written on Post-it notes stuck to the board at the front or on the walls around the room. You can either have the topics facing forward so they can read them, or facing backwards so it is a blind choice. You could call up students one at a time to choose or have a free-for-all.
- Topics hidden in places around the room.
- Topics hidden under their keyboards so wherever they have chosen to sit that lesson has selected their topic for them.
- Topics with other teachers – if you are linking up with other subjects, the students could have to find and speak to the other teachers. If a teacher of another subject has given out all of their presentation topics, the students will have to find another teacher on the list.

✎ **Lesson Activity:** *Debates*

Rather than giving a solo presentation, a way to get students really fired up is to introduce an element of competition. By turning the presentations into debates, not only do they have to argue rather than just present but they will also not be stood at the front by themselves – their opponent will be there as well.

Possible topics for debates could be based on current affairs, school issues or issues your students will be interested in. Allocate a student who is for and one who is against and allow them 5 minutes each to put across their argument, then 2 minutes each to counter the other's argument, and then perhaps allow questions from the audience.

Topics could include:

- reality TV is the most popular type of programme
- schools should continue to have/introduce a school uniform
- our school is 'green'
- there are very few lead female characters in computer games
- computer games promote or encourage violence
- studying Maths is worthwhile
- printed books are redundant
- we don't need high street shops when we can shop on the internet
- university the best path for a successful future.

🦘 **Lesson Activity:** *Presentations Without PowerPoint*

The phrase 'Death by PowerPoint' has become almost a mantra in business, where this program has been overused and badly used for so many years that some companies are banning its use altogether. Although this is one of the staple programs that students should be aware of, they should not think of it as the be-all and end-all of presentations.

Try setting your students a challenge to carry out a presentation without using PowerPoint. You may get some who use other software, which will develop their skills in these other areas. Some may not use ICT at all, and that is perfectly fine if you are assessing them on their presentation, although you should ask them to justify why they have not used it. Presentations are all about getting the message across and ICT should only be used when it is useful, not because it is there. Some may choose to just speak to their audience, some may use props, some may create a short drama piece, some may use drawings or a flipchart. Once presentation software is removed, the scope for creativity is huge and this is certainly an exercise worth doing to show that reliance on computers is not always necessary. Having an ICT teacher say this can provoke some interesting reactions! Often students will be so used to teachers saying their own subject is vitally important, it will be refreshing to them for you to say that it is useful when it is useful, but there are alternatives. (Obviously only do this if your class are already convinced of the importance of ICT!)

Spreadsheets

Every subject has certain areas which teachers do not look forward to teaching. It is inevitable there are always going to be parts where promoting enthusiasm and interest in your students is going to be difficult and where learning will be challenging as they struggle with difficult concepts. In my experience, working with spreadsheets is one of those areas. Therefore it is very important to consider how you approach it. Whether you are worried, bored or otherwise, you need to demonstrate with your language and body language that this is an important topic and that it will be interesting. You may also wish to start the topic by explaining why spreadsheets are useful – I find the argument that 'it does Maths for you' goes down very well!

⤵ Lesson Activity: *Topics for Spreadsheets*

As it is likely that your students will be working on their spreadsheets over several lessons, make sure you choose a topic which will excite them. Often they are given topics such as a mobile phone shop, which may seem 'cool' and 'with it' but it's really not and becomes very boring very quickly, almost as soon as they're told the name of the shop (and if that's Mobiles R Us, just forget it now!).

Possible topics could include:

- sporting events such as the Olympics or the World Cup – there are lots of data available on the internet about countries, teams and individuals which would provide scope for working with formulae and analysis of statistics
- calories in food, especially food they eat regularly, like fast food – this can really provoke thought!
- a small local business, perhaps one inside the school – a tuck shop, uniform shop, school canteen
- a business they can all relate to – pet shop, farm, zoo, restaurant, bus company, taxi firm
- using data from other subjects such as Science, Food Technology, etc.
- creating their own business idea.

Databases

The teaching of databases is changing in secondary education, as is evident in the new qualifications released in 2010. Database units have changed from the central purpose being creating a database from scratch to now focusing on searching data stored in a database and printing out the results. Whereas before students were expected to create the whole database, now they generally only have to know how to search and operate them for ICT user qualifications. The argument is that unless students are going to study further or work in the field of ICT, they will never need to know how to create a database – just how to use existing ones. However, this section is included as most schools and all sixth forms and colleges will have ICT qualifications for future ICT practitioners and will therefore need to cover databases in detail.

➥ Lesson Activity: *Topics for Databases*

Inventing topics for database activities can be difficult as database software does not lend itself automatically to exciting topics. It can be seen as a 'serious' piece of software, excellent for business but not exactly thrilling when it comes to teaching it. However, a topic that will maintain interest throughout the project can make the whole process that much easier.

Possible ideas could include:

- Completely free choice of topics, meaning that students will pick something which interests them. This will result in all sorts of topics such as shoes, MP3 players, horses, football teams, celebrities, films, Santa's reindeer, etc. Supporting this free choice can at times be tricky, as you need to be able to quickly get your head around each student's topic so you can advise and assist. I would suggest that this option is taken only if you are confident with databases.
- Cross-curriculum link-ups with other subjects, for example databases on elements for Science, on food stuffs for Food Technology, on volcanoes, hurricanes, world landmarks, countries or counties for Geography, on monarchs for History, etc.
- Something which is useful for the school. Perhaps even have a competition where the winning database will actually be used. This could include databases for the library, the school canteen, the health and safety officer or another area of the school. Although databases are ubiquitous now, there may still be areas within your school which could benefit. Make sure you get the agreement of the person your students will be making the database for and that you manage the size of the system, as there is no point in asking students to make a database which is too time-consuming.

➥ Lesson Activity: *Data Types*

Data types are sometimes a stumbling block when students are designing their databases. Often the idea of fields as categories of data is easily grasped, whereas assigning each of these fields a data type can sometimes be difficult. Therefore this activity aims to reinforce the principles of this.

Before the lesson, type up a list of several fields such as StudentID, Title, Firstname, Lastname, Address, Postcode, TelephoneNumber, EmailAddress, Age, DateofBirth, FavouriteSubject, Attendance%, LikesICT?, AdditionalNotes. Print or photocopy a few sets of these, each onto different coloured papers. Also collect several buckets (or similar) labelled with the different data types, such as autonumber, text, number, date/time, yes/no, memo (see this book's companion website for resources).

In the lesson, ask your students to form teams and give one set of coloured fields to each team. Place the buckets around the room. The teams' task is to place the right fields in the right data-type buckets. To reduce the chance of cheating (looking at what other people have put in the buckets) and to make them think quickly, give them a very short time limit, such as 5 minutes.

> When setting time limits, as you are the one watching the clock, you do not have to be strictly accurate. If you feel students are not working as hard as you would like, give them a time update every minute, but cut those minutes short or warn them that there is not much time left. If students need more time, secretly extend the time so they can all finish the task. If you are challenged on your time-keeping, say, 'We are going by my watch', or shrug and say, 'Perhaps my watch is running slow.' Bright students will realize you are giving extra time for fairness.

Once the time is up, go around to each bucket, lift out the slips, and read them out. Ask students to vote as to whether they think each one is right or wrong. Keep hold of the fields which are right in your right hand and those which are wrong in your left, or ask two trusted students to follow you around, one to hold the correct answers and one to hold the incorrect. At the end, count up the correct ones for each team (identified by the colour of the paper) and announce which team(s) got the most correct fields.

Extend this activity: You could repeat this activity for other sets of fields you have prepared. Alternatively, you could use this as a start or plenary in subsequent lessons. As they have done the activity once, it will be much faster to organize them to do it again.

Lesson Activity: *Queries*

Queries are often one of the most tricky areas of using databases. One of the main problems is that students will not have used them before and therefore do not have a context in which to put them – however, they *have* used them before without realizing! They will use databases all the time, every search on the internet uses a database, every time they browse products on a website, every time they use the school's VLE – these are all databases. Therefore they *will* have used queries before and will have a basic understanding of their purpose and function if this is pointed out to them.

A good way to demonstrate queries, and also promote databases and show why they are useful, is to show your students what life used to be like before computers. Before the lesson create a large set of cards, each with a record on. You could make one set which will be used to demonstrate to the class, or a few sets for three or four groups to see who can search it the fastest. Hand-write the records, perhaps even making some difficult to read, on cataloguing cards or something similar; you should aim for at least 20 cards so it is not too simple. Fasten them together in a random order either by elastic band or in a box.

In the lesson, ask a student to come to the front (if using one set of cards) or distribute the sets among groups in your class. Explain how these cards are a database, with each card as a record. Ask them to start with a simple sort – put the records in order (alphabetical by surname, date order or similar, depending on your data). This may take some time; allow them to invite other students to help them. When completed, point out that it has taken X number of students X number of minutes to do what a computer can do in seconds. Challenge them to try to do the next task as fast as a computer. Ask them to search for specific things, such as for a database about people, those with blue eyes, those older than 18, those with names beginning with F, etc.

Templates of these cards have not been provided on this book's companion website as this demonstration has much more impact with hand-written cards. If they are printed, even with handwriting-style fonts, it can give the impression that perhaps they were made on computer in the past. Using actual handwritten cards ensures this demonstration has a much stronger effect on the students.

⇨ **Extend this activity:** You could also make a quick database with the same data in it and have a race to see which version, cards or electronic, can search the data faster. Alternatively, once they have completed the tasks with the cards, ask them to carry out the same sorts and searches using the database and compare how much faster it is.

For an example database with accompanying worksheets in the style of a 'whodunit', see this book's companion website. To make it even more accessible to students, you could alter the data within the database to refer to teachers in the school, students in the class or celebrities.

Problem-solving ICT

By using a problem-solving approach to ICT, you are asking students to fulfil a brief, rather than learn a particular piece of software. For example, rather than a unit on spreadsheets, you may do a unit on managing a business. This means that students do not associate certain programs with certain tasks, but are able to see a problem and decide what is the best tool to solve it. The plus side is that they become more confident in their approach to ICT, less reliant on software from a particular company and more creative in their solutions. The downside is that you cannot guarantee which skills they will learn, specifically. In a spreadsheets unit, you can be sure that they will all learn how to create bar charts in a spreadsheet program, as there will be a criterion stating that they must fulfil this. However, in a unit on managing a business, they may choose a number of ways to display their data – they may choose a bar chart, but then they may choose to create something in a presentation. They may even make an animation to communicate their data.

Issues with problem-solving ICT

There are many ways to solve a problem, and there will often be different solutions which are equally valid. The question is: is there anything wrong with this? Must all students develop an identical set of skills, or is it equally valid for all students to learn how to solve problems using ICT? In the real world, they will not be asked to create a bar chart in a specific spreadsheet program – they will be asked to display their data clearly. Is the purpose of school to teach them specific skills or to prepare them for real-world situations?

There is also the issue that if students are using different tools to solve a problem, how can they be assessed equally? If one student creates a bar chart in a spreadsheet program and another creates an all-singing, all-dancing animation, can these be assessed equally? What about the student who always opts for the easiest solution? Can they be marked on whether the problem is solved? How do we develop a gradated marking scheme to award high and low marks with this? When are the skills learned in order to solve these problems – before starting them or while students are carrying out the project?

The main issue with problem-solving ICT is maintaining equality in terms of delivery and assessment. The problems given to the students would need to be very carefully tailored in order for them to have parameters in which to solve the problems, thereby somewhat limiting the vast range of responses that could be possible. There is a movement towards this in vocational qualifications where a problem is set with narrow parameters. For example, the problem 'Design and create a 2D cartoon' can only be solved using animation software, although any program of this type can be used.

There is also the dilemma that teachers would need to support the wide range of solutions being produced, one minute helping with a spreadsheet, the next with an animation. This asks a lot of a teacher who may also be tackling behavioural issues at the same time.

A solution to the issues of problem-solving ICT

There are positives and negatives to both skills-based and problem-solving approaches to ICT and the debate about which is best will probably continue for a long time to come. However, there is a third option, which is to combine the two approaches in an attempt to get the best of both worlds – students learning the skills first, then attempting to solve problems using the skills they have learned (this is discussed further in the section on skills-based ICT (page 43).

A problem-solving approach creates the fantastic opportunity of combining topics or units for vocational qualifications. Often units are very separate, focusing on specific areas. However, by combining these you can create a scenario which better matches the real world and also reduce the amount of time needed to teach it. For example, if you have units on using ICT for business (including creating a document and a presentation) and creating a website, you could combine these. Your scenario would be for one business for which your students create a business plan and an accompanying website. The presentation might be to launch the website – each part of the project uses similar information that is applied to different skills to produce the three distinct products. Even easier to combine are multimedia units for example computer graphics, animation and web design could be combined into one project, something more akin to the real world.

Problem-solving ICT activities

The following problem-solving activities allow for a range of responses. You may choose to use them openly and allow for creative solutions; they are easily adaptable to suit your particular requirements. Alternatively, if you would like to use them to specifically target certain skills, you can limit the parameters of response. Each project can be done individually or in small teams.

⤷ Lesson Activity: *Organizing a School Trip*

Brief: To organize a school trip.

Tasks:

1 Research possible school trips for your year group, select five and present your findings clearly.
2 Select one of the trips and create an advertisement to be shown in school (print or digital).
3 Cost the trip, taking into account (if applicable) travel, accommodation, admission prices, food, etc. Calculate the cost per student if all students in your year group took part in the trip.
4 Create a document to send to the parents of the students asking for permission, stating the cost and describing the trip, including what the student should bring with them.
5 Record the students who have signed up to go on the trip, whether they have paid, and whether they have been granted permission by their parents.

⤷ Lesson Activity: *Dragons' Den*

Brief: To invent a new product and put forward the proposal to a panel of judges.

(For more information on this activity, please see this book's companion website.)

> ⚐ This activity could be turned into a competition, with the best idea winning a prize. Also, a local business could get involved, perhaps giving a small prize or vouchers for the best idea.

Tasks:

1 Invent a new product – this could be something for school, something which the student has a need for, something which will fill a gap in the market, a new ICT/Media product or a new version of something which already exists.
2 Put together designs of this product or (for ICT/Media products) make a demo of this product. (As the product can be anything, these could include drawings, explanations, designs, short films, mini-websites, etc.)
3 Construct a business proposal for your business and your idea.

4 Create a presentation to put forward to a panel of judges. Once you have delivered the presentation, answer questions from the panel to further explain or justify your idea.

> ⚑ This panel could be made up of teachers, IT technicians, students from other classes or year groups, or members of the local business community.

Programming

Programming is an area of ICT that is often missed in education, maybe because it seems too difficult or maybe because it is seen as being too geeky for general users. However, programming is a crucial part of ICT and one which can give some students the spark of genuine interest in the subject, one which might persuade them to study the topic in more depth in later qualifications. It is useful to give students even just a small taster of programming, just to see if they are interested and to show them that computers don't work by magic – someone had to code everything that they see and do. The introduction to programming could be run as a couple of one-off sessions, perhaps at the end of a term, or maybe in extra-curricular groups.

When choosing your approach to programming, remember that you need to pick something which is accessible and can be learned quickly. Pick a visual language, like Visual Basic, or find a program which will provide you with 'chunks' of code or script for the students to slot together. Don't launch them straight into C++! You could consider some of the starter games programming software which allows them to grasp the purpose of the programming easily and also adds a dimension of creativity. VBA (Visual Basic for Applications) is also worth considering. Adding programming to Microsoft Office documents and spreadsheets can show that programming is useful as well.

When starting this topic, skip the usual first program, 'Hello World', no matter how tempting it might be to follow in the traditional footsteps of programming, and go with something which will have more impact. Remember your students will be used to visual stimuli and live in a media culture – try to give them something which looks impressive. Your aim is to have the students shouting, 'Cool!' once their first small program is complete. When they see they can create something 'cool', that will be enough motivation for them to try the next task and spur them on to continue learning.

Be under no illusion that teaching programming is easy, although with the range of software and languages that are now available it is certainly much easier than it used to be. The crucial thing is making it relevant and useful. If your students can see they are actually producing something constructive, even if it's as simple as making a sprite walk across a screen, they will be interested. When I was first taught to program (in the ancient, creaking language of BASIC on an Acorn computer), one of my first tasks was to create a diagonal row of asterisks across my screen. It took almost all lesson to accomplish and at the end I just looked at it and thought, 'What was the point of that?' Even though I had probably learned a lot of foundation knowledge about the language, my initial interest in programming had been lost. It was only when we started making programs which I could see had a practical use that my motivation returned.

> For some students the leaps of logic needed for programming or control of a language may be too much. You may want to put your students in pairs; if so you need to decide carefully how you will match them. If you put the strong, interested students with the weak, disinterested students, they will have an influence on each other but you can't be sure whether it will be positive or negative. This would be the one occasion where you could consider pairing weak students together; weak students with medium ability will also make a good mix – it depends on the mixture of your class.

If you go further into programming with your students, differentiation can become crucial. Be prepared to stretch those who want to go further and who are finishing the tasks quickly; have extension tasks ready to give them extra challenges, even if it is just a casual comment of, 'Why don't you try making it do X?'

For weaker students, consider how they will get help. There is no point in you doing it for them, no matter how tempting that may sometimes be. You could prepare helpsheets to give them when they cannot follow the instructions. These could take the form of blocks of code which they need to enter and put in the right order, or a missing words exercise where all the code is there but with some words missing or even tasks written in pseudocode.

Interesting starter, refresher or plenary tasks can include:

- students are given printed pieces of code and an objective and work in groups to put the pieces of code in the right order
- students write pseudocode (which may then become their plan for the program they make)
- students are given incomplete or incorrect programs (either written or on computer) and asked to complete or fix them.

Multimedia

Multimedia used to be an 'add-on' to ICT, yet now it is a core part of most curricula, with whole qualifications being dedicated to this specialist area. It is a very exciting area in that it allows students to combine their ICT skills with high levels of creativity. They can produce amazing results and I find that this is the area where students surprise me the most. Some will approach a brief from an unexpected angle; some will invent a detailed idea that they have obviously spent time thinking about and working out; some will adore this area of ICT and spend hours and hours doing their set work and creating their own pieces. For some students who have previously dismissed ICT as boring or difficult, introducing multimedia can grab their attention and suddenly they can be top of the class or want a career in this field.

Multimedia can draw students into ICT: if they are not interested in the 'harder' logical areas, this 'softer' creative area can really get them interested in it. It can also lead them directly into the harder areas, for example students who enjoy computer games and have made sprites and backgrounds for a game may then be more willing to try programming it to work. Students who take photographs and edit them may then enjoy turning them into a presentation or putting them with some data in a database.

A small word of warning before you start a multimedia task – time is a crucial factor. These sorts of activities can grow into monsters and before you know it you are spending extra lessons on it which weren't in your scheme of work, especially if your students are really into it and putting a lot of effort in – it is always a shame to stop students when they are interested. When you plan your multimedia tasks, give your students a deadline from the beginning. This not only hands the responsibility of time management to them (a skill which is vital for them to develop) but also simulates real life where multimedia projects have set times and do need to be completely finished for a specified deadline. Lay it on thick that they must meet the deadline – perhaps the 'client' in your brief needs it by that date if you have included one in your scenario, whether real or fictitious. However, set your deadline at least one lesson before the actual deadline, leaving yourself flexibility in your scheme of work. If all students have finished on the deadline you have told them, use that extra time for them to peer review each other's work or present their products and explain how they work and why they have made it that way – you could even persuade a member of staff to act as the client and give feedback, or pick a winner (the product that the client would pay for and use). If they have not finished, give them an extension to the actual deadline, but really make a point that you are going out of your way to give them this extension, that it would never happen in the real world and that they MUST have it completed this time. While students will think you are very generous in giving them this extra time, you had allowed for it all along and it does not take time away from other lessons you had planned.

When planning schemes of work, always leave yourself flexibility. You never know when you will lose a lesson due to a power cut, school closure from adverse weather or students going out on a trip that you were unaware of. Leave at least one lesson per topic free, but have an idea of what you can do in these lessons if your students do follow your planning. Prepare some ad hoc lessons that you can pull out at any time – standalone lessons that are ready to go if you find yourself in the luxurious position of having spare time.

Multimedia is sometimes seen as a frivolous area, but the skills developed are genuinely needed for the students' future careers and personal lives. Remember that the skills we teach them in ICT are not just advantageous for their impending higher education and employment, but also enable them to fully take part in modern society. It is increasingly true that multimedia is being taken seriously as an element of ICT that is genuinely needed for students' futures. Even jobs where these skills would once not have been needed now require young people to have these skills, for example web design. Employees may not have to design a site from scratch, but may be expected to edit a company's existing one to keep its information up to date. Virtually all companies have websites but not all of them have web developers to look after them and look to their staff to maintain it.

In all areas of multimedia, design and planning are key. This could be very formal and involve prepared templates, such as storyboards for animation or video, or it could be a matter of giving the students pens and paper and asking them to sketch or mind-map their ideas. Do not underestimate the creative potential of big pieces of paper and marker pens. Also, if students want to work on the floor, let them – let them be creative and try a new space in which to think of ideas. In creative lessons, your room may become organized chaos; it may look chaotic to outsiders looking in, but always remember the 'organized' part and that you are in control.

Multimedia is a good opportunity for group work, something which is often veered away from as it is difficult to assess an individual student's work when they produce a collective product. However, in the real world multimedia products almost always are created in a group environment and the success (or otherwise) of a project depends on that one final product.

For all projects in multimedia, see if there is a real-world project which your class could undertake. For example, is there a local event coming up for which your students could create a website or an animation to be shown at the event? Speak to local businesses – do they need anything? Consider libraries, museums, art galleries, tourist information centres and other organizations which may appreciate your students' help in this area. Students benefit immensely from real projects as they not only see the purpose in what they are doing, but also have the challenge of creating something which may actually be used by someone else.

Digital photography and graphics

Digital photography and graphics are the core of multimedia because all of the other forms (except sound) use skills from this area. For example, when creating a website one can use photographs and other images.

The key message about digital art is that it is the one area in ICT where it doesn't matter how the final image has been created – what matters is that the final outcome looks they way the artist wants it to look. There are often several ways to achieve a desired effect, and students can some-times be surprised that the simplest method is often the most effective. The starting image is important; if working from their own photographs, the better they are, the less they will have to do to it. They need to be reminded to keep it simple and not to over-edit.

There are many programs which can be used for editing graphics – choose whichever is most suitable for your students and your school's budget. The expensive programs are industry standard and will prepare your students for the types of programs they may use in the future; however, they are generally very large and you will never have time to show them all the tools available. If you are giving students a lot of freedom, you may need programs which will do lots and lots of things; however, if they are working on quite small projects, perhaps a correspondingly sized program would be more suitable. There are cut-down versions of larger programs available at special educational prices and free software available under the GNU licence on the internet. See this book's companion website for suggestions and ideas.

➡ **Lesson Activity:** *Topics for Digital Photography and Graphics*
Some possible topics for photography and graphics you may like to consider using include:

- Design your bedroom – give students a picture of a bedroom, either one which is very old-fashioned or one that is very plain. Ask them to decorate the room such that they would be happy to have it as their bedroom. They must keep the structure of the room intact, but can change any other aspect. They can use original photos or images from the internet.
- Faces – give students a selection of high-quality images of celebrities and ask them to merge them into one. Use one image as the main image, and move over the eyes, nose and mouth of the second image. Then use tools to combine the extra parts so it looks (vaguely) like one person. Sometimes the results are impressive, sometimes they are hilarious and sometimes they are positively inhuman, but students have great fun doing this, especially when celebrities of the moment are used.
- Proverbs – give students a proverb and ask them to create an image of it without using any letters or numbers. They should take at least one original photograph and include it. This gets them really thinking about their image and the symbolism in it.
- Representing the abstract – give each student an abstract word such as 'love', 'hate', 'freedom' or 'truth' and ask them to create an image to represent that word (without using any text). An interesting way to do this is not to reveal the purpose of the task and to ask students

to go and take photographs around the school for 10 minutes. Then when they come back, give them their word and ask them to pick one of their photographs to then edit and represent their word.

Also consider combining this topic with another, such as web design, as they fit together really well. The images will then have true purpose as they will go into web pages and the students will develop two sets of skills in one project.

If there is time in this topic, it is valuable to do one lesson on how to take photographs. Consider the following components:

- composition
- rule of thirds
- viewpoints (this is a really significant one as students will automatically take all of their photographs from their standing height – by suggesting they crouch down or stand on something high and look down it can instantly make their photographs more interesting)
- framing the image
- foreground and background balance
- perspective
- moving vs. static objects
- lighting.

Web design

In web design, students make web pages, incorporating text, graphics, hyperlinks and other elements with the aim of creating a cohesive website. Projects can range from a very small site with three pages to something much more complicated with at least six to ten pages. Generally if students make more than ten pages, not only does the site begin to get unwieldy, but they will be repeating themselves and the extra pages will only mean more work rather than further development of skills. If they really want to do it, warn them how much work and time it will take – don't stop them, as they may surprise you and you don't want to stifle their enthusiasm, but suggest that they get the core pages done first, so that if the extra ones are not completed, at least there will be enough to mark and for the student to get a good grade.

Web pages can be built in a simple text program by writing pure HTML but it would be advised to use something with a graphical environment, preferably WYSIWYG so that what they create on screen is exactly what would be shown online. There are large programs that are industry standard and will allow students to develop strong skills which they will be able to use in the future; however, this software tends to be expensive, is sometimes tricky to operate and takes time to learn. If the web design project is a full-sized project which will take a reasonable amount of time, students will have time to learn the intricacies of the software and operate it successfully. If it is a short project, perhaps something smaller and simpler may be more appropriate, including software which is freely available on the internet. See this book's companion website for suggestions and ideas.

➥ **Lesson Activity:** *Topics for Web Design*

Some possible ideas for web design you may like to consider using include:

- Completely free choice – this allows students to create websites about something which interests them, meaning that they should be more enthusiastic towards the project They will also not need to worry about learning about the subject; they should already have the content and can concern themselves about the design and compilation of the components of the site. Allowing free choice can leave room for foolish or dodgy suggestions – perhaps ask all students to submit their ideas or designs to you for approval (as the 'client' or 'web team leader') to ensure you remove anything that may not be appropriate.
- A new business idea – ask students to invent a new business idea. Perhaps it will be similar to one that already exists and they think they can design a better website for it. Perhaps it is a business website they use and want to create their own version of, or perhaps they have spotted a gap in the market and want to create something new.
- Many websites for one business – give students a business, e.g. sweet shop, museum, local radio station, new band or musician. Every student must make a website for that business. You could persuade another person to come in and pose as someone from that business, e.g. the little old lady who owns the sweet shop, the museum curator, the local radio DJ or the musician/band (if you find a volunteer with theatrical leanings, they can really go to town on their character and bring the project to life). The students could interview their 'client' and also take photographs of them to be included. There could also be props they could take photographs of, or a trip could be organized to their business's location.

When doing web design, students are very likely to ask you whether their work will be put on the internet. This is something your school will need to decide. It might choose to make them available for other students to see via the school's VLE or they may choose to link to the best ones from the school's website, which means that the students' parents/guardians can see their work – a really positive thing for both students and parents/guardians.

If there is time in this topic, it is valuable to do one lesson on HTML. Start by explaining how tags work and relate the '<head>' and '<body>' sections to the human body: inside the head is where all the thinking happens, whereas the body is the part you see. Show students a simple web page and either give them pieces of HTML to rearrange into the right order or ask them to write the code on paper or into a program to re-create that web page. Another useful task is to ask students to print the HTML for their completed website and annotate the tags to describe how it works. This can make a nice wall display if stuck to large pieces of coloured paper and annotated in large colourful words.

Animation

Animation is the creation of short movies or cartoons – it is essentially creating graphics and running them over time to see the images change. It is useful to give students background on animation, talking about how cartoons like *The Simpsons* are drawn, how claymation works and how long (and how many people) it takes to make full-length animated movies, perhaps comparing older classics like *Snow White and the Seven Dwarfs* (a hand-drawn film by Disney) with modern computer-generated films. Then, when you ask students to make a short animation, perhaps 1 or 2 minutes in length, they won't think you have lost your mind setting them a task to create such a short animation.

There is expensive software available for this area which, unusually, is fairly simple to use; however, there are cheaper and free alternatives available on the internet. Again, choose the software which is best for your students (and your school's budget) and see this book's companion website for suggestions and ideas.

➥ Lesson Activity: *Topics for Animation*

Some possible ideas for animation you may like to consider using include:

- A story about a character – you could either give your students a character or they could design one themselves. They must then animate the character to tell a story about it, consisting of a beginning, middle and end. It is worth pointing out to them that humanoid characters with limbs are quite complex to animate and, if they would like something similar, considering using blobs and shapes with faces, which they can move in interesting ways and also still get effective facial expressions.

- The Olympic Games – ask each student (or group) to create an animation about an Olympic event and then compile them into one film. For students who finish early, their extension tasks could be to create the opening and closing sequences. Their clips could be funny or they could be serious. Working towards a collective goal as a class can spur them on as they support or challenge each other, lending a competitive (therefore productive) atmosphere to the class.
- An upcoming event – create animations based on an upcoming event or season, such as winter, Halloween, summer holidays, the school's birthday, sport's day, the school play. The animations could be used to show to the whole class or to other students as part of the event, e.g. animations about the school play could be shown by the entrance to where the performance is taking place (without giving away the storyline!).

If there is time before students start using software to create their animations, ask the students to create an old-fashioned flip book, where on each page they draw a different picture, slightly different from the one before so that when it is riffled the images look like they are moving. The first image must be drawn at the back, then the next on the second-to-last page (using the previous one to trace if needed) and so on. This could also be set as a fun homework exercise.

Sound

Sound involves different types of recording:

- voice recording
- sound effects recording
- music recording.

Sound can be used in other multimedia projects, such as animation or web design, and while this area is often not covered as a standalone project, there is certainly enough depth to it to warrant its own slot.

There is expensive software available, but there is also free software which is just as good and very easy to use. However, if you are planning to record and edit music, more complex software may be needed, depending on how in-depth you wish to go – your Music department may already have some software that they may let you use. See this book's companion website for suggestions and ideas.

➥ **Lesson Activity:** *Topics for Sound*

Some possible ideas for sound you may like to consider using include:

- Podcasts about the school – students could record descriptions about the school or anecdotes about certain subjects, teachers or events. If suitable, they could be put on the school's VLE or website.
- Radio documentary – students could record personal stories about what has happened in their lives that week or accounts of interesting things that have happened to them.
- Radio play – the students' recordings could be of a fictional story. They could also add sound effects to give it more atmosphere.
- Sound effects – give your students an animation with no sound – one which is quite abstract or has a story – and ask them to create the sound effects using Foley techniques, such as coconuts for horseshoes, recording footsteps on gravel, and running water.

If there is time, perhaps for homework, students may enjoy creating a 'mash-up' where they combine two quite different songs.

Film

Film is a medium which students instinctively understand, as they have usually been exposed to a great deal of imagery on television, in films, on the internet, in shops, and even sometimes just walking down the street.

Your students will need to work in groups as film-making is something which is very difficult to do individually. They may choose to get other people involved as 'actors', in which case remind students that they must seek permission from the people involved to be in their films and not to force people to be involved. It may also be worth you reminding your staff that if they are approached to be in your students' films they should not feel compelled to take part if they do not want to.

Video cameras can be expensive, but there are some which are relatively cheap and film in a suitable quality. It is also often very easy to transfer the footage from the camera to the computer for editing. In terms of software, there are some very complex programs available which are suitable for those wanting to go further into working with film but, for ICT projects, using free software will give you all the tools necessary to compile an effective, interesting film. Please see this book's companion website for suggestions and ideas.

⤷ Lesson Activity: *Topics for Film*

Some possible ideas for film you may like to consider using include:

- Filming a narrative – give students a short story or script, something they have not seen before, and ask them to create a short movie of the story. They may do it literally and act it out, or they may go for something more abstract and conceptual.
- Music video – ask students to select a song and create a music video to go along with it. They may choose to dance to it, interpret the words or use more random imagery.
- Movie trailer – either give students a description of an existing movie or ask them to come up with one themselves, then film the trailer for it. They could investigate the key elements of a trailer including:
  ~ generating interest in the film
  ~ showing off the stars in the film
  ~ suggestion of cliff-hangers, genre, atmosphere
  ~ information such as production team and release dates.
- Charity advert – allocate a charity to each group of students and ask them to create an advert for the charity to persuade people to donate to their cause. The adverts could then be shown to another class and then voted on to determine which is the most persuasive and to which they would donate.

Computer games design

Computer games design is a large area with many elements involved including narrative, animation, graphics, sound and programming. Introducing games design to your students is likely to get them very interested, especially if they can produce games which they can get their friends to play. It is such a big area, it would be quite easy just to teach games design and in fact there are qualifications available to do this (and many university courses and employment routes if your students wish to take this career path). However, it is likely that unless you teach specialist courses you will not have the luxury of enough time to do something really in-depth. Nevertheless, it is still a valuable area for your students to study.

Because computer games design is such a huge area, it would be impossible to make a large-scale game in class, but it should be possible to make a casual game, similar to *Tetris* or *Pac-Man*. There is some excellent software available, mostly free, which can be used in class to make these simple games. It is generally designed for children or hobbyists and therefore is very easy to use.

You could give a character to your students or they could invent their own, and then create their own game ideas. They are bound to show a wealth of creativity and will likely come up with a whole range of interesting, exciting game ideas. Depending on their level of ability, you could ask them to start creating their game from scratch, making their sprites and backgrounds and putting in the code to make it work. Alternatively, you could give them a start for each of their games. If you do this, manage your lessons so that they invent their own game ideas at a time that gives you a chance to put together the starts of their games (e.g. before a quiet week or a holiday). Create just the start of the game using average-looking sprites. From there students can first re-create your version, then improve the sprites and finally improve the script, perhaps adding another level, another baddie, another pick-up or whatever may be needed in their game.

When creating games, to make sure they understand their code rather than just getting it to work through trial and error (which is a good method, but does not ensure comprehension), you could ask them to print it and annotate it, highlighting exactly where things happen.

2

Other Elements of Teaching and Planning ICT

As well as teaching the subject, ICT teachers have other areas that they need to consider. Some of these are the same as for other teachers, such as assessment and dealing with challenging pupils and tricky areas of the curriculum. However, there are elements which are peculiar to ICT, such as the design of the classrooms, which often involves ICT teachers being called on to give their expert opinion as the people who most use the rooms.

Assessing ICT projects

The assessment of ICT work can be difficult, because the easiest method of assessment is the marking of written work or answers to exam questions. Because ICT does not lend itself to that very well, there is a debate over the best assessment methods for the subject.

The written method, used in academic qualifications, may require students to sit an exam and provide written answers or write an essay-style answer. This type of assessment is good for measuring students' theoretical knowledge and fundamental understanding, but it does not give them an opportunity to demonstrate their practical knowledge. Some projects may require students to carry out a practical task and take screenshots as they do, explaining at each stage what they have done and why. These are easy to assess as they can be printed. They are, however, overly laborious for students to perform and can also be susceptible to cheating and do not truly demonstrate a student's practical abilities.

The practical method, used more in vocational qualifications, requires teachers and students to provide assessment materials in a different way.

Rather than writing about a topic, students may be asked to deliver a presentation and be filmed; or they could be asked to create a film as the assessment tool. Students may be given a practical ICT task, such as creating a spreadsheet, and the product they create is the item that is assessed, rather than documentation and screenshots accompanying it. This method also lends itself to teamwork, which is an important skill students need to learn but also one that is generally not assessed or even encouraged in qualifications. However, there are issues with this in terms of proving that the work is the student's own. In addition, providing consistency across all marking can be difficult – it is easier to say whether two written answers should obtain the same number of marks as opposed to two animations. However, as a lot of vocational qualifications have introduced these methods of assessment, standardization is possible and feasible.

Unless you are restricted by an exam board's choice of assessment method, use as many different methods as you can. Each method will work to different students' strengths: some may prefer written answers, some may prefer giving presentations, some may prefer submitting a practical piece of work. In other subjects they may spend a lot of their time producing written work and ICT is a good opportunity to allow them more freedom and to try something different. You may even give them a choice – to submit their work they may produce a short film or audio recording, for example. Some methods may not only assess the topic they have been working on, but also give a refresher of other topics (such as presentations). Look out for opportunities to combine areas of study like this. Just remember that it is your duty to ensure fair and consistent assessment of students' work at all times.

I'll let you in on a secret – first impressions do matter. Whether it be submitting a project to a teacher to mark or to an exam board, the appearance of the project, the accuracy of the spelling and even the quality of the printing will have an effect on the assessment. Teachers, assessors and moderators are trained not to take these things into account – after all it is the subject knowledge that is being marked – but it is impossible to ignore the presentation. We are only human, after all! It is your responsibility as a professional to mark all work fairly and equally; however, you can certainly help your students to produce the best piece of work they can in the time they have *before* they submit it for assessment.

In ICT, you will often find the word 'appropriate' in assessment criteria, e.g. that the formatting the student has used is 'appropriate'. This is quite a subjective area and one which often causes debate and disputes when assessing work. Although it is often easy to spot inappropriate uses of ICT, there is a fine line between 'appropriate' and not. There is also an habitual assumption made that students know what 'appropriate' is. It must be remembered that virtually all of your students will have no business knowledge, will have not seen professional documents and will not know what is appropriate. They may be quite happy to include pretty clipart pictures dotted all over their formal, serious business letter because they think it makes it more interesting and attractive to read; however, we know, as adults, that this would not be appropriate.

However, the word 'appropriate' will continue to exist in ICT criteria, so it is our responsibility to help students understand what this word means. A good, simple method is to show them examples. Bring in copies of professional letters you have received, show them a copy of your CV, or perhaps show them a copy or mock-up of a spreadsheet you might use to look after your personal finances – obviously removing any private information from all of them first!

Also, ask your students to consider the user in every possible context. A key word in ICT is 'communication' and as such they should always remember that they are trying to convey information. Pose the question, 'If you showed a manager of a business/your parent/the head this document, would they understand it?'

What do all these grades and levels mean?

Attainment levels, letter grades, passes, merits and distinctions . . . what do they all mean? How can you work out what grade each of your students should be given? You may hear experienced teachers saying, 'Oh, he's an A student, she's on a C', before they've marked their work. They seem to be able to do it from just looking at their students, but in their classes they will be watching each of their students and noticing the signs.

It is all based on how much effort they are putting in, their enthusiasm, the questions they ask or contributions they make to class discussions, if they ask questions when they don't understand, and their engagement. Ability is also a factor, but teaching is all about raising ability levels and is itself something that can be improved. I was once asked in an interview what sorts of students I liked teaching; I replied, 'It doesn't matter what they have done or what they can do, as long as they're willing to try' (which received nods and smiles – and I got the job). If a student is willing, and malleable like plasticine, a good teacher can mould them into a high achiever. If a student is resistant, it is still possible, but you first have to break down the barriers before you can start shaping them.

In ICT, it is not usually the technical elements which decide a student's grade. When doing a project on spreadsheets, they should all be able to physically carry out all the required formulae and functions. It comes down to whether they can explain it and how much they actually understand it. Have they planned it? Can they explain why they have done each bit the way they have? Are they able to evaluate their work objectively?

How can you spot a student who can achieve top grades but who is currently achieving bottom grades or failing? How can you spot the students whom you can get more out of, the ones who would benefit from a little more of your precious time? Honestly, it's in their eyes. This isn't some sort of 'windows to the soul' idea, but there are two easy things which you can watch out for and which will tell you immediately how engaged your students are.

1   What do they look at? While you are explaining something, talking to the class, giving instructions, what are their eyes focusing on? If they are looking at you, your board or a worksheet then that shows they are engaged with what you are saying and are willing to put effort into the lesson. If they are looking at their computer screen and can hardly take their eyes of it, or when you ask them to stop working to listen to the next instruction they keep going, they are engaged with the subject. Perhaps their behaviour and focus need a bit of work, but they are clearly interested and want to do the work. This is something you can work with. If they are looking at other students, reading the posters on the wall, staring into space – they are not engaged. Watch for the crafty students who look like they're looking at you, but are just staring idly and not really receiving what you are saying.

2   Do they have a sparkle in their eyes? Can you see life in their eyes? Students who have that gleam of life, spirit, character and personality visible in their eyes are the ones that you will easily be able to do something with. Even if the glint is telling you that they are up to mischief, it means they are engaged with making mischief and are willing to put work into making mischief – you can turn that around and get them engaged with the subject. The sparkle tells you that there is something about that young person – there is energy, interest, there is 'oomph' – and you can use that and turn it towards your subject, your teaching, their learning and their achievement. Students with dull eyes can gain a twinkle and you need to find the thing that makes their eyes sparkle. Every student has something that interests them.

Next time you go into a class, look around at their eyes and you should see that interested, focused, sparkling eyes will belong to those students whom you can identify as producers of good work or as being capable of doing so. If you know about this 'early warning system', you can make quick assessments of new classes, which can then be augmented as you get to know each of the students.

How can you resist the pull of being generous to the ones who have always worked and paid attention to you? At the same time, how can you resist being harsh with the students who haven't worked, who have disrupted others and who you know did their coursework the night before the deadline? You have to remain objective. Even if you have built good, professional relationships with your classes and genuinely care about them and are committed to doing everything you can to help them achieve highly, you MUST NOT let this affect your marking. Even if you are under pressure from your school to produce good results, for league tables or for your reputation as a teacher, you MUST NOT let this affect your marking.

First, don't let the student's behaviour or personality cloud your judgement. You are only marking the work, not the effort. If you know the student has not done any work all year and then slogged through the night for the past week, that is not relevant. If you know the student has prevented other students from achieving because of their behaviour, that is not relevant either. Nor is the knowledge that the student has struggled with bullying, illness and difficult parents relevant. You are only marking the work. If you are able to, do blind marking (when you do not know which paper belongs to which student). Maybe ask a colleague to put sticky notes over each name. Part of being a teacher, a professional, is being able to remain completely objective. This is all very difficult, and we all fall into the trap every now and again. If you feel you are likely to adjust the marks on certain students papers, whether positively or negatively, ask a colleague to second-mark it and see if they get a similar result. Always remember that coursework for qualifications will be moderated, meaning the marking is checked by others (sometimes called 'work scrutiny'). Internal moderation is usually done within your department. External moderation is done by exam boards and might involve a moderator visiting or posting work to the board. With both types of moderation, work is usually randomly selected and marked. If it is found that your sample is above or below for certain grades, the whole set of coursework might be remarked or the exam board may choose to adjust all students in your school up or down a grade for that unit, as appropriate. Having had that happen to me once (due to an ambiguous criterion in the unit specification), believe me, it feels awful and is something to be avoided at all cost. Therefore make sure you can hand-on-heart say that your marking is fair and accurate, and always moderate internally before submitting work for external moderation.

Second, if you are working to a specification, National Curriculum or a framework, make sure you follow every word. I would advise the following method:

- Copy the whole spec into a word processing program.
- Colour-code each section. For example, with Pass, Merit and Distinction, I change the font colour to red, yellow or green respectively.
- Delete any duplicates. For example, if the student has to 'save the file with a sensible name' for all three criteria, delete the Merit and Distinction ones, as this is something which is needed in order for all students to gain a Pass.
- Press enter at each full stop to put each sentence onto separate lines.
- Find each 'and', then press enter to put each of these sentences onto separate lines.
- If any line looks too long, find a point where you separate that into different lines as well.
- Read each line – if any contains more than one criteria, break that into separate lines as well.
- Reorder the list so the colours are together, lowest at the top, highest at the bottom.

You should end up with a list of things to achieve and what is needed for which grades. For a student to achieve the lowest grade, they need to do all the things in the first colour. For a student to achieve the highest grade, they need to achieve everything on the list. This can now be used to create a project to work through and also for marking. Also consider putting this in a format which the students will be able to follow and give each one a copy. If they know exactly what they need to do for each criterion, they can take ownership of their work and understand that grades aren't plucked out of thin air – it is genuinely dependent on whether they do X, Y and Z.

Making the 'boring' bits fun!

In ICT, as with every subject, there are certain topics which are, I'm afraid to say, boring. There are always parts that some students will like and others will not, that is inevitable. But every subject has its 'stinkers', parts that teachers dread because they know it's going to be a fight to keep their students awake, much less interested, and because students won't get it the first time, they will have to repeat them over and over, which compounds the problem.

Usually in ICT, these topics are the ones which do not relate directly to practical computer tasks; the ones which are about information, such as researching, legislation and health and safety. You may be greeted with this question at the beginning of the lesson: 'Are we going on the computers today?' If your answer is no, you could immediately be faced with belligerence and disobedience, unless you can come back with this kind of answer: 'No, I have something even more fun for you today.' The best way to deliver these topics is by making them enjoyable for both you and your students, and by ensuring the message sticks with them the first time you deliver it.

If there is a topic which makes you anxious, worried or exasperated, your natural instinct will be to try to get through it as fast as possible. In fact, you should be doing the opposite. If you are worried about delivering a particular topic, it is likely because it is difficult to learn, whether that be due to the abstract content or because students find it uninteresting and therefore put in less effort to learn it.

If you don't enjoy a topic, neither will your students. Teaching and learning is a shared experience and your approach to a topic or a lesson will affect their attitude as well. If you show that you dislike a part of ICT, your students will dislike that same part. You may have seen this in action already. You announce that you are starting a certain topic with a class and they all moan – how can they have this attitude without ever studying it, unless you have subconsciously (or consciously!) planted the notion in their heads that this particular topic will be boring? Enter your classroom brimming with enthusiasm, free from stress, happy to see your students and looking forward to the lesson ahead. It doesn't matter whether any of this is true – your attitude will make a difference and hopefully become a self-fulfilling prophecy. The more you enjoy teaching, the more your students will enjoy learning. If you are bored, they will be bored. Every teacher must be an actor and their classroom their stage.

How to deal with challenges

Although teaching is the best job in the world and while there are many positives, there will always be elements of the job which you do not look forward to. No job is perfect, but teaching tends to be more polarized than most, giving you real high points but also low points that sometimes make you question yourself and your choice to do this difficult, rewarding job for a living. It can be an emotional roller-coaster.

The high moments can be small and personal or great and visible. From the simple breakthrough of a student finally understanding a concept, saying thank you or deciding to behave appropriately in class, to watching your students pass out of school with qualifications they have worked hard for into places at university or employment, to seeing them win honours such as playing for a junior national sports team or winning an award – at every opportunity, look at your students, whether they are gathered for class, assembly or just milling in the school grounds, and think what awesome potential each of them carries. Take pride in their achievements, celebrate with them, congratulate them – no matter how big or small.

There is no disguising, however, that there are also the low points. It might be a particular topic, a certain class or a task such as that pile of marking that will come in at the end of term and take over your holiday. The best way to approach these is with optimism and a strategy.

- With that difficult topic, if you find it hard or boring, so will you students. Therefore arrange your lesson activities to be varied and fun, and lead them through the ideas slowly, with lots of time for reflection and repetition to help them understand. Don't be tempted to rush through it, to get it over and out of the way. There is always a reason why you are teaching the topics you are, whether set by your school, the exam board or as part of the National Curriculum. Every tiny element of a curriculum has been scrutinized and argued over, ensuring it is the best, most useful it can be. Give each topic the time and respect it needs.
- For that difficult class (and you will always have at least one), start every lesson as though it is the first time you have seen them and tell them how good this lesson is going to be. Have patience with them and do not settle for second best. If you expect them to be silent when you speak, wait until they are silent. If they interrupt, then stop, wait for silence and start again. If they keep interrupting, pander to their curiosity: 'If you decide to let me finish this sentence, you will find out what exciting task we are going to do today.' As well as optimism,

have a strategy. Know what you will do if they take certain actions. Have your rewards and sanctions ready. Two which work very well are:

a) Praise good behaviour and ignore bad behaviour, making a point of lavishing attention, smiles, kind words, house points, or whatever system your school may use, on the students who are good and also stating that you will do the same to those who also behave well (ask, 'Who else can I give a gold star to today?' as you look around the class, catching the eye of the worst offenders). Being allowed to leave the lesson a little early is also a good reward as students always value time. If your school is strict on lessons lasting their allocated time slot, it could be just a couple of minutes early, or perhaps it could be keeping the others in a few minutes. It is a powerful demonstration when the well-behaved students exit the classroom first, leaving the others behind.

b) When you need to use your school's sanctions, if it is low-level misbehaviour, you could use 'three strikes and you're out'. If you introduce this, explain it at the beginning and make sure your students know what behaviour will earn a 'strike'. For the first strike, the student is informed of the behaviour which is incorrect and how they could correct it – and their name is written on the board. If you need to ask them again, they get a second strike – underline their name and make sure you remind them that their third strike will receive a sanction. For the third time you need to ask them to behave, put a cross next to their name and apply whichever school sanction you feel is appropriate (if they need to calm down, send them out of the room; if they need penalizing, give them a warning, remove house points or send them to speak to a head of department, whichever is the first level on your school's discipline system). Make it very clear what they are receiving the punishment for and how they could have avoided it. They have broken your agreement and you have no choice. Once they have had their punishment, start them off again at zero, saying that you have faith that they will turn over a new leaf this time and prove that they can behave.

– For that arduous task, like that mountain of marking you've been dreading, have a strategy. Allocate time to complete it and establish where you will start and where you will end. I know this sounds obvious, but when you are faced with large or multiple tasks it can sometimes become overwhelming. We always ask our students to manage their time effectively, plan realistically and prioritize their tasks, yet we can sometimes be the worst offenders. Even if we think students don't notice this, they do and we must be good role models at all times, including when managing our workload. Break that pile of marking down into manageable chunks, perhaps do five papers a day, or five papers an hour, depending if you are the type of person who likes to spread it out or blast through it in one sitting. Give yourself a reward at milestones and at the end, even if it is just a cup of coffee and a biscuit. If you feel like you are flagging, stop – there is no point slogging at it if you are not going to do a good job. It is unfair to the students to mark the first half of the papers well and the second half not so well because you are tired. Take a break, watch some television, go for a walk or decide to tackle it later or tomorrow.

Planning an ICT room

If you are fortunate enough to be in the position of planning the design of an ICT room, there are many options available to you. Unlike other classrooms, whose layouts can be rearranged, an ICT room is fixed and therefore it is imperative that the chosen design is the best one available.

The first thing to consider is the purpose of the room. Will students be working individually or will you want to encourage group work and collaboration? Will they just be using computers, or will they need space to write or put books on the table? Will the room need to be suitable for exams? If so, there is a whole host of regulations which need to be considered. Will the room be just used for lessons, or will it be open access for students to use in breaks, lunchtimes and after school? Will students always be supervised in the room? If the computers are accessible, will they be tampered with? If they are not accessible, how will students plug in headphones or USB devices? Will it just be ICT teachers using the room, or will non-ICT teachers be using it as well? What atmosphere do you want the room to have: technical, relaxed, industrious, professional? Will this room be one which is shown to visitors – does it need to be visually impressive?

With all aspects of a new room, especially an ICT room, consider the health and safety regulations which may be applicable. Ensure that key people in your school are involved in the process from the start, including your health and safety officer, senior management, Maintenance and IT Support.

There are several standard table layouts available and the choice is dependent on the room which is to be used, the number of students to be accommodated at one time, and the desired feel of the room. The chosen design needs to make best use of the space, without causing overcrowding. Be wary of wasted corner spaces, where desk space cannot be used because chairs and computers cannot be fitted in. Also remember to consider the positions of printers; they need to be in accessible positions (so printouts can be retrieved without disrupting the work of students or leaning over them).

Classic desk layouts

Classic layouts include:

- The U-shape, where the desks are lined around the edge of the room. In this layout the computers are facing towards the teacher, meaning that it is possible to see what every student is doing on their screen at once. However, all your students will be looking away from you, which can impede the relationship between the teacher and student, and also means they have to keep turning round to see you or the board.
- The M-shape, where desks are lined around the edge and up the middle of the room. This design is very good for getting the maximum number of computers into the room and if large class sizes are an issue, this could be the best solution. Similar to the U-shape, the students do not face the teacher; however, in addition to this, the teacher cannot see all screens at once. There are only two positions where screens can be seen: in the open space at the base of each arc in the M. Students will soon learn that when you are stood in one side of the M, you cannot see the other side's screens. I would only recommend this shape if there is no other way to fit the required number of seats into the chosen room.
- The E-shape, where desks are set out in rows across the room, similar to a formal old-style classroom. In this arrangement, all students are facing the front all the time; however, you cannot see what is on their screens until you move to the back, meaning you move away from your presentation equipment at the front and, by the time you move to the back, students will have removed anything inappropriate (such as games) from their screens. They can hide behind their monitors so they are difficult to be seen from the front as well. It is possible to get specialist computers and desks to suit this style of layout, where the computers are sunk into the desks and students look down onto the screens. However, for students who may need to sit at the computers for a long time to write coursework, this is not the most comfortable arrangement and does have health and safety issues.

Contemporary desk layouts

As well as the classic layouts, there are more contemporary ones, including:

- Circles, where each desk is triangular and the desks are arranged in circles, usually seating six or eight per circle or 'pod'. This is creates a warm atmosphere and one where students will feel inclined to collaborate, although it lessens the temptation of looking at the next screen as it is slightly angled away and would take more than a glance to see it. In this arrangement, there are always some students facing the front, whose faces you can see, and some who have to turn, but you can see their monitors and therefore get the best of both worlds. In addition, panels can be made to slot between each desk to make them individual and suitable for exams. This layout is very good for producing a 'non-classroom' feel, a different space in which to learn.
- Columns, where desks are in rows but vertically down the room instead of horizontally (as in the E-shape). In this layout students face outwards from the middle, meaning the teacher has a good view of all computer screens from a central position at the front and students only have to turn 90 degrees in order to see the board. This design is space-efficient and produces a 'classroom' atmosphere, a formal space in which to learn.

Other elements of an ICT room

Once the layout of the room is decided, all of the other elements can then be chosen:

- Computers: Will they be above or below the desks? How will headphones, USBs and CD drives be accessed? Just as a side note here, I have seen schools which have put their computer base units in a separate cupboard to clear the desk space and to prevent tampering. However, the problems which ensued ranged from students turning each other's computers off accidently to the computers overheating when the air conditioning was turned off. I would advise you to stay away from this solution.
- Chairs: Rigid plastic chairs are long-lasting and cheap, but are they comfortable? Fabric chairs are comfortable, but will the hydraulics survive fidgety students? There are tamper-proof chairs available, but at a price. Always consider health and safety regulations. Think carefully before purchasing chairs with wheels – do your students really need them or will they cause innumerable problems including

collisions in the classrooms and races in the corridors? Chairs which are normally sold with wheels can usually be purchased with glides instead.

- Cables: All computers needs cables and electricity so make sure you take this into consideration. The last thing you want in your impressive new ICT room are trailing cables making the room look untidy or dangerous. Are your computers near the walls? In which case, do you need more sockets installed? If the computers are not near the walls, how will they connect to the power? Will you run the cables under the carpet? If so, how will the cables be protected; do you need grooves cut into the floor under the carpet? Will you run the cables in the ceiling, in which case how do the cables get from the computers to the ceiling? Will you use pipes to hide them away and will this affect visibility?
- Air conditioning is an important part of an ICT room as it prevents the computers from overheating – and the students too! Where will the control panel be? Will students be allowed to use it? In addition, consider any radiators or opening windows which could conflict with the system. Will it be just for cooling or will it completely manage the temperature in the room?
- Lights are very important. In an ICT room, you must always consider the effects of glare, from sunlight through the windows and from overhead lights. Consider installing specialist anti-glare lights which are standard in rooms where computers are used. Also think about installing blinds. Can the room be darkened in order to show a video clip? If possible, have split lights so those at the front can be turned off and the board can be clearly seen, while the lights at the back remain on so students are able to see to make notes.
- Consider where your projector will be and whether it will be a normal projector (which can produce a shadow and shine brightly into the eyes of the person at the front) or a short-throw projector (more expensive but eliminates problems of normal projectors). Will you have a normal whiteboard which can be used for projecting and writing, or will you invest in an interactive whiteboard? There are devices available which will allow you to turn a normal whiteboard into an interactive one cheaply and simply, and are also transportable to other classrooms when needed.
- Where will you locate the printers? What about storage? Do you need lockable storage for equipment or students' work?
- Consider control software which enables you to view all students' screens from their computer and allows you to take action such as banning specific websites or programs, taking time-stamped screenshots

of students' screens as evidence of their being off-task or blanking all of their screens so they are not distracted while you are talking.

Teaching ICT without a computer

ICT does not always have to be taught in an ICT classroom. This may seem like a radical statement but, just as other subjects sometimes move into the ICT room to learn, likewise you can move out. There are many opportunities for ICT lessons without computers and, if used in moderation, they can provide poignant moments of learning. Think back to your school days – some of your best lessons, the ones you remember most clearly, are the ones where you did something different. You can create those lessons, the ones that your students will be reminiscing about when they are all grown up.

Leave the ICT room

Some of the activities given in 'The basics' section of Chapter 1 (page 17) include activities which could be run outside the ICT room, either in other rooms and spaces or outside. Also consider other opportunities that will enable you to teach away from your normal ICT classroom. Is there a lesson where you will be discussing an issue or teaching a topic where the students will not be using a computer? Not only will the different location make the lesson more interesting, but it will remove the 'When are we going to use the computers?' question which is almost like the 'Are we there yet?' of long car journeys. If there are no computers, students can't be distracted by them.

Consider other rooms and locations such as non-ICT classrooms, the theatre, the sports hall, the dining area, outside sitting on the grass (in the summer), and all the other interesting places you will have in your school.

If your students are doing a lesson on planning, such as storyboarding for an animation, move them into the theatre and give them big sheets of paper and marker pens. In this creative space, they may feel more free to come up with new, different ideas – and it will also stop them trying to create their animations before they have completed the planning.

Consider holding business-style meetings. For older students, move to the dining area and provide coffee and biscuits and get them to hold a meeting, just like is done in the real world.

Perhaps start your lesson in one location, then move to another, and then maybe back to the ICT room to enact the planning or decisions that have been made in the first half. Alternatively, start your lesson in the ICT room and then move your whole class to another space, perhaps to indicate a change of topic.

Make sure you take a register at the beginning of your lesson, no matter where you are, and again if you have moved locations, even if it's just a quick silent count-up in your head to make sure your whole class has arrived. If you are worried about losing students in moving around, ask someone to help you out and bring up the rear, perhaps a learning assistant or IT technician. They will only be needed for the 5 minutes it will take to move your class from one location to the other and ensure they are all there.

Leave the school

When it comes to school trips, almost every subject will have options. They will have events which are perfectly suited to the areas being taught, places which will have a standard trip for subjects each year, some which are even specially put on for school trips – but ICT is often considered to be a subject for which trips are not possible. English has plays they can watch, Art has exhibitions they can visit, PE will have away fixtures, Geography might do all sorts of exciting things in all sorts of weather. However, just because there are no standards for ICT yet established, do not be discouraged as there are many options for trips and visits in this subject. Trips in ICT can alter students' views on the subject, may enhance their work or may even encourage them to study ICT further, and perhaps to pursue a career in the subject.

Please do not let the barrage of paperwork or legislation surrounding trips deter you from running them. Work with your health and safety officer – they will be a fountain of knowledge and be able to help you complete any forms needed. The experiences students gain on trips, even just short visits, enrich their learning and their school lives. I once took a group of students to the local library where there was an art exhibition of local artists. One of the students, a 16-year-old boy with a bit of an attitude, sidled up to me as we entered and explained how he had never been to an art gallery before. He spent the next hour excitedly moving from picture to picture pointing out the details, examining them closely and wanting to discuss each piece further with others in the class. He came away from that new experience enriched, a tiny bit more mature and his creative work showed a new perspective and depth – and he would talk about that afternoon as one of the most fun things he had done at school.

Ideas for ICT trips and visits

The key to a fun and fascinating outing is keeping it relaxed, having clear learning objectives and behavioural rules, and making it useful. It is always best to run a lesson directly before the trip in preparation for it, outlining what they should look out for, perhaps giving them a worksheet to complete while they are there and having them discuss what they think they might learn. It is nice to give students free time while at a place (if it is suitable), but make sure the educational section of the visit is completed first and then whatever time remains can be free time. If the morning has been interesting, perhaps they will think about it, or even talk about it, in the afternoon. If you are with them, perhaps you can throw questions about the morning into the general discussion to keep them thinking about it. Consider the following ideas for trips:

- Places which are set up for school visits and will also provide educational talks, discussions or experiences. They might even tailor their services to a subject which you are learning on request. These include museums and interactive visitor centres such as Sellafield in Cumbria, Centre for Life in Newcastle, the National Media Museum in Bradford, Eden Project in Cornwall or the Science Museum in London.
- Experiencing ICT in a real-world environment, perhaps one your students may not have considered. Most ICT projects talk about ICT in the office; however, ICT is used absolutely everywhere. Venues can include theme parks, supermarkets or department stores (seeing behind the scenes), airports, the local radio station, cinema or bowling alley.
- Comparing how ICT is used in an office environment, in which several of them may work in the future, visit both a small business and a large business. Visiting ICT-based organizations can also be very interesting, especially for students who wish to work in the ICT industry in the future. This could include businesses who manufacture computers, design websites, create software or even computer games studios (although because of the privacy issues concerning the games they are working on, sometimes this can be difficult to organize.

- As the basis for a project. This could be making something for the venue, such as a program, database or spreadsheet, or using the venue as a topic for website design or the creation of business documents like leaflets and letters. These places could include a zoo, a town or city, a leisure centre or a local council.

When students are carrying out more creative projects, for example using multimedia (see page 63), you could take them for short visits, perhaps for a morning or afternoon, which can provide inspiration or just a new space to think. Fresh air is great for clearing the mind and allowing ideas to flow in. Such visits could include:

- art galleries, especially less formal, modern or local galleries
- a walk in the local park, by a river or just around the nearby streets
- historical houses, interesting buildings or local beauty spots which are close to your school.

There is also the option to travel outside the UK, and there are several companies which will organize residential, international ICT trips to other countries. Destinations could include Paris (e.g. Disneyland Paris), New York or Prague. These are able to be booked with reputable school travel companies who will organize transport, accommodation, talks and other events.

All of these sorts of excursions can greatly benefit your students. They may give them a new perspective on the world of ICT, or they may be inspired to produce more creative products.

> ☞ Key to any activity outside school is the establishment of clear rules and expectations before setting off. All students involved must know exactly how they should behave, what will happen if they break the rules, and why those rules are important. If students understand why they have been asked to do something, they are much more likely to comply. The rules should be explained to them at least the day before the trip and then again when it is about to commence. If you explain the rules when they are in mufti, excited and ready to get on a bus, the message will not be received and remembered.

What to do when the power fails

It is inevitable that at some point you are going to walk into your ICT classroom or be teaching in there and suddenly – nothing. It could be a problem with a server, perhaps a network cable has been severed by workmen, or it could be a power cut. These are things you just cannot plan for, but you can be prepared. Unlike other classes, who can generally function without power, and may not even realize there has been a power cut if the sun is shining through their windows and they are using textbooks, pens and paper, in ICT you will know immediately. The important thing is not to panic. If you have some tricks up your sleeve, you can shift seamlessly into another activity, as though you had planned to do it all along.

If your students were working on the computers at the time, hopefully they will have saved recently so as to not have lost too much work, but reassure them that you will ask your IT technicians to attempt to recover as much as they can (never make any promises as they might not be able to retrieve unsaved work). This will serve as a good reminder as to why it is important to save regularly!

During these downtimes, your school policy is likely to be to keep your students in your classroom until the situation is rectified or until you are given more information. It would only be in the case of a serious power cut (or other environmental issue) where you would be required to assemble your students in a central area, where they might be kept until more information is known or until parents are able to collect them. You will be told if this is to happen. Therefore, you need to be prepared to continue teaching without computers or anything electrical. If you have prepared for these situations, you will be able to carry on, keep control and reduce the temptation of your students to misbehave by keeping them occupied.

➥ Lesson Activity: *Ideas for Keeping Students Interested during Downtime*

For short blips in the network or power, don't over-react. It's only when you know it will be prolonged that you should move on to a different activity and stop waiting for the situation to be rectified. You could try to continue teaching through other activities but, if we're realistic, your students will see this situation as an excuse to stop learning and misbehave. Your main objective is to prevent them from misbehaving. Just asking them to sit quietly and still is never going to work. Even the best-behaved students will begin to get at the very least fidgety. Using your discipline methods will also generally not work because they will view this subconsciously as not being part of the lesson and therefore assume that normal rules do not apply. The best way to keep them calm is to keep them interested, by introducing what you will do as, 'Let's play a game!' Some of these games may seem a bit frivolous, but they will help you keep control of your class during this time of forced inactivity, and they will practise essential skills such as quick thinking, communication and teamwork, which are vital in your subject and all others.

> **o—** Always remember that even though your primary task is to teach your students ICT there are transferable skills which they should be developing at the same time, and also life skills which will become invaluable in the future. Every time you ask them to write, verbally describe or plan something, they are developing skills which they will use throughout their education and career. Just because it may not be in your criteria to assess spelling or presentation of work, always remember that these are important skills. You do not need to make a big issue of it or change their grade, but on work which has been submitted, note where they could have improved or return it to them to improve before resubmitting.

Playing *Hangman* and *I Spy* can be good for staying with an ICT theme, but they are a bit old and tired. Try something different to keep your students involved and therefore behaving. These games can be played as a whole class, but by introducing the element of competition, your students will be more focused and involved, especially if you have a prize (which you could provide in the next lesson). The following are some ideas you might wish to consider using:

- Play charades in teams, using titles of movies, books, music (songs or artists) or video games. Either you can write down titles in each category to give them to act out, or you could ask all of your students to write something down, drop them into a 'hat' and then pick one out at random and act it out to the class who could either be in one team for fun or two teams for competition.
- Picture charades is where students are asked one at a time to come to the board and silently draw something using a board marker. The rest of the students should try to guess what it is. To add an element of competition, students could be in two teams and a member from each team is asked to draw the same thing at the same time and the

team who guesses it first wins the point. More fun can be added by
blindfolding the 'artists' or asking them to close their eyes.

- Write one long word or phrase on the board, perhaps the name of your
school, and challenge your students in small teams to form as many
words from its letters as possible in a set time (perhaps 10 minutes).
Introduce rules such as the words must be four letters or more and no
proper nouns are allowed. At the end, teams could swap, count up,
argue over which words are allowed, and work out the winner.

- Ask a student to come to the front (or one from each team) and secretly
tell them an object. They then have to describe that object without
saying any of the words in its name, e.g. they must describe 'black bird'
without saying the word 'black' or 'bird'.

- Ask a student to the front, give them a topic and ask them to speak on
it for a minute without repetition, hesitation or deviation. The other
students can listen carefully for slip-ups and they can enjoy catching
each other out.

- Ask a student to the front and ask them questions – they must answer
without saying 'Yes' or 'No'. Try to catch them out with questions like,
'Do you like ICT?', 'Do you think the power will come back on soon?',
'Are you having fun?'

The worst-case scenario for this sort of situation is a power cut when it is
dark outside. Unless your room is fitted with emergency lights, you will
likely be plunged into darkness. The first thing you should do is to instruct
all of your students to remain in their seats and stay quiet so they can
listen to your instructions. You should keep two battery-powered torches
in your desk drawer in case this happens (one to use in the classroom and
one in case you or a student needs to leave the classroom to find more
information or visit the toilet) – regularly check that your batteries are still
functioning so are ready. If you are in darkness, you can still continue to
control your class and teach them transferable skills – don't let a little thing
like complete blackness deter you! Keep your ideas with your torches in
your desk drawer.

Lesson Activity: *Ideas for Keeping Students Interested during
a Power Cut*

When you have to teach in darkness, your aim is to keep your students
calm, in their seats and paying attention. As noted in the previous Lesson
Activity, you do not have to keep teaching ICT – any activity you do will
develop their transferable skills.

Tribal Camp

Hold a 'tribal camp' discussion where only the person holding an object may speak – perhaps the torch. The discussion could be about the topic they have been studying, or it could be something else, something which keeps them engaged and interested. You could let students voice their own opinions or split the class in two and have a debate. Make a rule that the person holding the torch can only say one sentence before it is passed to someone on the other 'team'. Topics which will get them fired up and involved could include 'Women are less intelligent than men', 'Football is for idiots', 'It is more important to get a job that you enjoy than one that pays well', 'What job would you like to do and why?', 'If you won the lottery, what would you do?'

My Fantasy Job

You could start the creativity element of this by telling your students an outlandish real or fictional job you wanted to do when you were younger.

Alphabet Game

Play the Alphabet Game, where each person takes it in turn to say a word starting with the next letter of the alphabet, e.g. apple, banana, cherry, etc. Topics could include fruit, vegetables, places in the world, celebrities' surnames, computer games, animals, etc. There is likely to be debates over certain answers as to whether they are allowed so be prepared to be a referee, although remember that if they are producing coherent arguments (as opposed to just arguing) they are using important verbal skills and it might be interesting to let them reason it out themselves. Those students who get Q, X and Z might need a little help or be allowed to cheat a little. Full lists can be found on this book's companion website to help you.

The Minister's Cat

Play a game which has been around since Victorian days – the Minister's Cat. Each person takes it in turn to say, 'The minister's cat is a . . . cat', filling in the blank with an adjective beginning with the next letter of the alphabet. For example, 'The minister's cat is an adventurous cat', 'The minister's cat is a beautiful cat', 'The minister's cat is a curious cat', etc. You could make it more relevant by changing it to the Headmaster's Cat or the Naughtiest Kid ('The naughtiest kid is an angry kid', 'The naughtiest kid is a boisterous kid', etc.).

Nanofictionary

Play Nanofictionary, where your students will make up their own story by taking turns. You can choose whether they take turns saying a sentence or just an individual word. For students who like the limelight you may wish to put a limit on the maximum number of words in a sentence (e.g. ten or twenty); for those who are not so keen, give a minimum of two. It may take a little to get into it, but once their imaginations are fired they can produce some wild and outlandish ideas, which will keep the momentum going. They may also start to try and catch each other out by leaving difficult endings for the next person to continue. You could start everything off by saying, 'Once upon a time . . .'

Also remember that in a total power cut your heating or air conditioning might also have been affected. Always remember health and safety comes first and keep your students warm or cool as needed. If your room becomes too cold and it looks like the power cut will last for some time, lead your students to a warmer room, perhaps joining with another class. Make sure you take a register when you arrive at the new location to ensure you have not lost anyone along the way.

3

ICT as Part of Other Subjects

There is always going to be some crossover between subjects. English and Maths are commonly found in other subjects, and you may even see a bit of Science in History (in topics like the history of medicine) and a bit of History in Science (when discussing famous scientists and their discoveries). This interweaving of areas is inevitable in our current structure of separate areas of study because real life is not as clean-cut as the education system; in real life you don't say, 'Now I will do some Geography' – you may decide to go for a walk in the countryside (taking some Physical Education) and encounter interesting rock formations (Geography) and some old ruins (History); you may stop and have the packed lunch you prepared (Food Technology) and chat with your fellow walkers (English) and even sing as you continue your walk (Music). Cross-curricular activities happen in real life naturally, without really thinking about it, whereas in education it is contrived. However, in order for education to reflect and prepare for real life, cross-curricular activities need to occur and they also give students a richer learning experience.

ICT, however, is unusual in that it is the only subject that specifically *must* be used in every subject. This may be something formal, such as Functional Skills embedded into curricular which has specific critera,using ICT in teaching because it is looked for in inspections, or using it because it is useful – all of these scenarios acknowledge the fact that ICT is part of every person's life and career. I challenge my students to name a career which doesn't involve computers in some way, and so far they have not managed to find one. They will often suggest farming, but I ask them how do they think cows are milked and after a moment they realize that it is all done with machinery controlled by computers. They may not look like the computers we have in the classroom, but they are computers nonetheless.

Cross-curricular responsibilities
of an ICT teacher

As an ICT teacher you will often be called upon to support other departments' use of ICT. This might be as simple as being asked advice, or could be as involved as preparing materials or actually supporting in class. The level of assistance you provide will depend on your school's set-up (whether you have someone else who is designated to help other departments), your job description and your willingness to help. You may also be required to train other members of staff in improving their ICT skills, and you will find all sorts of levels of ability and varying levels of willingness to learn more.

There are typically three main types of people you will encounter. First, there will be some members of staff who are computer-literate and quite happy and confident using ICT in their teaching. The second type will not know very much about computers, just enough to get by, and may be quite scared of using them; they may be proud of the fact they can't use ICT or may whisper it to you embarrassedly in the staffroom. This type of person will need coaxing and reassuring to take small steps in developing their knowledge and be very wary of using ICT in their lessons as they will not want to look foolish or lacking in front of their students. Third, there are the people who have some ICT knowledge and think they know more than they actually do, sometimes showing off to other members of staff and either making them more worried and perplexed or demonstrating incorrectly and spreading bad ICT habits around the school. This type of person can be quite frustrating as they may be unwilling to learn or try to second-guess you as you are explaining something, going off on a tangent and causing confusion. With this type of person you need to be very tactful, and massage their ego a little to prevent them from becoming defensive. Rather than saying they are doing something incorrectly, suggest a 'better way' of doing it. The best approach when dealing with staff and ICT is to treat them like students (without them knowing you are doing so). Praise them, raise their expectations, slowly build their confidence, be tolerant, repeat an instruction if necessary, encourage them. As teaching professionals, they are all experts in their own subjects and therefore have vast knowledge in their own area – don't automatically expect them to be ICT experts like yourself as well. Be patient.

What is key to using ICT in other subjects is that it should not be used too much. There is so much pressure for teachers to use ICT that it might almost seem as though they are supposed to be using it all of the time. However, the more it is used, the less impact it has and the less it is seen as different or special. ICT should be used when it is appropriate, when it will support the teaching and learning, and when it will help the teacher and students and result in better understanding.

As an ICT teacher, or co-ordinator, you may be responsible for ensuring cross-curricular use of ICT. This is something which is required by all schools and an element of an inspection and is therefore not dependent on whether a teacher wants to use it or not – all teachers must use it. Equally, all students need to have an opportunity to use ICT in all subjects. Other responsibilities might include eSafety of staff and students, administrating a VLE and/or supporting its use by all staff and students, or managing or co-ordinating with IT Support. When you go to interviews, make sure you ask exactly what the job will entail and what responsibilities you will have over and above your teaching.

How other subjects can be used in ICT

When you think about cross-curricular use, you will likely mostly think about other subjects using ICT in their teaching and learning; however, there is also the option of other departments teaming up with ICT to jointly deliver curriculum. Although it takes a bit of planning and co-ordinating, the benefits are huge, including:

- being able to teach the ICT curriculum and another subject's curriculum more efficiently – the skills and knowledge taught in either lesson are reinforced in the other
- because the other subject is including ICT in their teaching, delivery is more diverse and is carried out with the support of an ICT specialist involved
- the students' ICT skills are being used in a realistic project and they can see the benefit of their learning in action.

At a simple level, cross-curricular use could be a combined homework, for example if students are learning about spreadsheets in ICT and about different types of fats in pastry in Food Technology, the two topics could be combined into a special homework where they enter the data from their Food Technology lesson into a spreadsheet and produce graphs. Make sure you agree beforehand which teacher the students will hand the work in to.

More entwined cross-curricular co-operation could deliver subject matter simultaneously, for example in Music students may learn about different composers across several lessons, at the same time in ICT they could build a database about those composers. In every ICT lesson they are reviewing their notes from Music and the database has real data in it.

At the end, the students could produce reports of the composers to take back to Music. The best way to find activities like this is to compare the ICT scheme of work with other those of other departments, or publish the ICT scheme of work, stating when you will be covering certain topics and invite departments to link up for cross-curricular delivery. Make sure you outline the benefits to their teaching to encourage their involvement.

See the online resource 'How ICT Can Be Used in Every Subject' on this book's companion website.

Managing an ICT lesson: A guide for non-ICT teachers

As teachers we develop a set of skills and a style which works for us and our students; however, when using ICT in a lesson some can be moved out of our comfort zone. Teachers with less ICT knowledge may feel intimidated and worried that they will not be able to manage their class effectively in this alien environment, the biggest fear being that the students will know more than them and they will be made to look foolish.

As an experienced ICT teacher myself, I've had to accept that some of my students will always know more about ICT than me. They have time to surf the internet and find the latest 'cool' internet craze and they are willing to experiment with new software and see what it does, without working towards a specific goal. However, this fact does not scare me – in fact it motivates me. As an expert in my subject, I know more than my students in most areas of ICT, but in a subject which changes so rapidly all the time, there is no way I could know EVERYTHING about ICT – it's impossible. I think it's exciting to walk into a classroom and find myself challenged with, 'Did you know that if you click here, you can do this?' Not only is this student really chuffed that they have found something that their teacher didn't know, but it also means that they are interested enough in my subject to spend their free time experimenting with it and that they have independently developed their own knowledge. Also, I can learn from my students and pass this new knowledge on to others. In doing this I always credit the student, which also gives them a confidence boost, saying, 'I know what would work here, Brett showed me it the other day . . .' Do not be scared by the students' knowledge of ICT – embrace it, learn from it, become more knowledgeable from them. Learning is always a two-way process – we as teachers can learn as much from our students as they learn from us.

Running a lesson in an ICT room

All the techniques available to a teacher are applicable in an ICT room. Just because a teacher and their students are in the different environment of an ICT room does not mean that the established behaviour rules do not apply. Follow normal procedure. If you take a register, do so; if you always wait for silence, do so; if you have a seating plan, enforce it – just because a student has logged on does not mean they cannot be moved – they can easily be asked to save their work and log on to a different computer. If you have all students logged on, swap badly behaved students with well-behaved ones so that naughty students will not only see that they have annoyed you, they will also see that they have annoyed the person you swap them with, as well as their new neighbour, who will hopefully not talk to them.

Be aware that it will be exciting for students to be taken to this different environment for this subject's lesson, especially if it is something which is only done sparingly in this subject. Use that excitement and make sure they focus their energies on the lesson, rather than allowing them to see it as an opportunity to misbehave. Clearly know your objectives for this lesson and plan exactly what will happen – this is especially important if you are not confident around computers.

Know your school's ICT room rules. Must students line up quietly by the door before being allowed to enter or are they likely to already be there and logged on by the time you arrive? Must there be no eating and drinking in the ICT room? How do you contact the IT technicians if you need them?

Asking students to look something up on the internet can lead to all sorts of websites being accessed – it might be wiser to give them a set of several websites and ask them to look at each one and compile their own description of the matter in question.

Be aware whether your school has filtering software and what that will mean for your lesson, and what the blocked page looks like so you recognize it when you see it. If students encounter a blocked site, don't ever try to circumvent the filtering software, just ask the student to find another website – there are billions of pages on the web and there will always be a better place to find the information. If the room has control software which can control the students' screens, practise with it beforehand and be ready to use it in the lesson – if students think you are unfamiliar with ICT they will be impressed by you using this and more wary about getting up to mischief.

Decide beforehand what you will consider acceptable and not acceptable, and what you will do about it if unacceptable behaviour occurs. For example, is it acceptable for students to check their email in your lesson?

It may be helpful to give them time at the beginning or end to do so, to remove temptation and to prevent them being distracted by email during the lesson.

Running a lesson using laptops

Many schools are now buying a set of laptops which teachers can loan for a lesson for students to use. If this is available, it means that an ICT lesson can be run in the teacher's ordinary classroom. Consider the positioning of the laptops. If the classroom is in a U-shape, decide whether students will sit around the outside so their faces can be seen, or in the centre facing out so their screens can be seen. In a classroom with rows or sets of double desks, will all the students face the same way, or will they sit alternately forward and backward? Is the purpose of using the laptops to work on an individual project or group work?

Other things to consider when using laptops include:

- Cables – laptop batteries should last for the duration of the lesson, but if they have not been charged beforehand, how might the students plug them in to the power? Will you need extension cables or multi-outlet adapters?
- Network connection – do the laptops need to connect to the school network for students to log on, access their work or use the internet? Is there Wi-Fi available in your classroom? How strong is the signal?

Ten tips for a lesson using ICT

1 Know beforehand how many computers are available and if you will have enough for your class. Maybe check with a technician that all are functioning correctly.

2 Have a back-up plan if there is a problem with the computers, such as network failure or a power cut.

3 Consider that sometimes students do not bring pens and paper to ICT lessons – either ask them to do so beforehand or provide them yourself.

4 Find the positions in the room where you can best see the students' faces and their computer screens. Take advantage of any reflective surfaces (such as windows if it is dark outside).

5 When talking to students, consider moving them away from the computers, perhaps to sit around a table, or gather them on chairs at the front of the class.

6 Get students logged on before you start teaching. If logging on takes some time or the software takes time to open, ask them to start the process then begin your introduction.

7 When a student needs help in the lesson, resist the temptation of taking their mouse and doing it for them. Unless it is very complex, use verbal instructions and point at the screen. If you do need to move the mouse for them, make sure they are watching the screen carefully. Undo your actions, then ask the student to redo them.

8 Remind students to save regularly throughout the lesson and at the end.

9 If they need to print at the end of the lesson, leave plenty of time for this. For a class of 25, a good 10 minutes is probably needed – longer if they are printing long documents or files in colour. If they all print at once, the printer's queue of jobs can become jammed – perhaps ask one half of the room to print first, then the other half.

10 Don't be afraid to ask your ICT teachers or IT technicians for help or advice.

4

ICT as a Leisure Activity (and How It Can Enhance Learning)

ICT is unusual in that you will be able to say almost definitely that all of the pupils in your school will continue their learning in your subject in their own time. Although English teachers can say pupils may read at home and History teachers can say pupils might watch documentaries, ICT is the only subject where you can be pretty sure that every single pupil will be furthering their learning at home. Don't imagine for one second that they are making spreadsheets for fun at home – it takes a very rare breed to do that (and yes I am one of those people) – but your pupils will be spending their free time using a computer, surfing the internet, chatting to friends, playing games – all activities which not only enhance learning in your subject but can also benefit others.

○━ Learning through play is a fundamental part of early years and primary education. Children are allowed to play and as they do so they do not realize that they are actually playing educational games, ones that make them read, write, count and think. Just because a pupil reaches the age of 11, or because they are preparing to sit qualifications, or because they are in the sixth form and are 'cool' does not mean that they want to stop playing. Even adults want to play. You will have been to a conference or a lecture where you were required to sit for hours on end listening to someone talk at the front. Just because you are an adult does not mean that this is an effective way of learning – we would never ask our pupils to do this.

Learning through play is one of the best tools in a teacher's toolkit. It's the one that will get pupils interested and enthusiastic and having fun without realizing they are actually learning. If you can introduce this into at least some of your lessons, they will be the ones which are enjoyable to teach, entertaining for the pupils and the one that will stick in their minds. Don't use it all the time, because then it becomes less effective – just drop these types of lessons in periodically, especially for topics which are dry, and it will spice things up a bit and rejuvenate your teaching and therefore your pupils' learning.

Leisure ICT at school

Are your pupils allowed to use ICT in their free time at school? Are they encouraged? How do they spend their time? Are they using their time constructively? Are they working or 'messing around'? Could this 'messing around' be beneficial to their ICT education? Can you develop this further?

Using ICT in free time at school

Pupils who can use ICT in their free time at school have a fantastic opportunity to further develop their computer skills in addition to the formal ICT lessons they receive, without really realizing that they are actually learning. This may take place at breaks and lunchtime, or perhaps before or after school. If your school does not provide this facility it is worth considering introducing it; however, to ensure it is a safe and robust system there are some factors you may wish to consider:

– **Supervision:** Your school may have a policy in which pupils must be supervised when they use the ICT rooms. If so, perhaps it doesn't have to be the ICT teacher who is present at all times (which would be a big demand on your time) – you could get other members of staff involved as volunteers, perhaps with a rota system, or even get the older pupils involved, e.g. prefects if you have them. Promote it as a positive thing, that it's an opportunity to work in the ICT room with guaranteed access to a computer, and maybe even use persuasive tactics, such as stating that those who supervise the room will have access to certain sites (e.g. social networking sites) and get extra printing credits as privileges – whatever your pupils value.

   However, if you have instilled in your pupils good ICT practice, and they know the rules and why they are in place, and you also have good website filtering and monitoring software, do they really need supervising as well? Might it be just as effective to have staff 'pop in' as they are passing to check the room, rather than having someone there constantly?

- **Behaviour:** Are you worried that if you have an 'open access' policy for your ICT rooms that they will become damaged? Will they eat and drink beside the computers, will they be rough with the equipment? Although it is valuable to allow pupils to use ICT in their free time, it is still your classroom and you should be able to walk into your teaching space and know it will be ready for you to use (just like other classrooms in the school). If this is a concern, then there is a possible solution that you can present to your senior management: next time the computers in your classroom are upgraded (which should be fairly regularly, about every three years), create an 'ICT Common Room'. Find a room which is available and set up that room with the old computers (which would have been disposed of, sometimes at a cost). This room can then be used by the pupils however they want, with the proviso that if a computer gets damaged it does not get replaced. If you make the room nice, a pleasant place to 'chill out', it will become a space where they chat with their friends, using the computers casually, perhaps to check their emails, perhaps to play a game. There could even be drinks machines in there, the one place in the school where they can take drinks near the computers. There may be a book swap, comfy chairs and music system. You have then created two very different spaces – one for casual computer use and one for education, with different behaviours expected in each one. Give the pupils the responsibility of looking after their area – perhaps allocate a prefect or responsible older pupil with the task of looking after it.

- **Too many pupils:** If you work in a large school, although you may have several ICT rooms you may be concerned that if they were 'open access' you would have too many pupils wanting to use them and there could be aggro over which pupils use them. Those who are pushy might get them all the time, disadvantaging the quieter or younger pupils. There are systems you could consider:

  - Allocating certain days to certain year groups, e.g. Mondays are Year 7 (breaks and lunchtimes), Tuesdays Year 8, etc. This way each year group has the opportunity to use the facilities without pressure from older pupils.

  - Have a ticket system, like a lottery, where each pupil has a number (perhaps using their official pupil number) and each day or week do a random draw for Monday morning break, Monday lunchtime, etc. An email could be sent to all pupils stating which ones have access that week. Those who were chosen could not be entered for the following week and then put back into the draw for the week after.

~ Use of ICT could be based on priority, where pupils state their intention, e.g. those who want to do school work get priority, followed by email, educational games, internet, etc. This would need to be supervised to ensure it was fair and that the pupils were doing what they said they would.

~ A booking system could be used where pupils can sign up to use a computer at a certain time and date. It could be a digital form on the school's VLE or a paper version outside the ICT room. This would work on a first-come, first-serve basis.

Using ICT in students' free time could be encouraged by competitions. These could be whole-school or targeted for certain year groups or ages. They could be set by you and the ICT department, the head teacher of the school or even the IT technicians. The prizes could vary, from internal school rewards such as house points, to recognition of their work being put up in a prominent place or actual prizes such as book vouchers or online music vouchers. The competitions could vary, from designing a poster for the school's 'green' campaign to researching on the internet for the answers to a set of difficult questions to creating a short video showing the best three features of the school.

If some of your pupils have free periods (perhaps the older ones), they may ask if they can drop in to your room while you are teaching. For some lessons this might be fine, but it can become distracting if you have a stream of pupils asking if they can drop in to a lesson where you don't want extra pupils in the room. It may be useful to put the timetables of each ICT room up outside each classroom. Mark the lessons where there is definitely no drop-in in red, those where there may possibly be drop-in (if they ask) in yellow, and times when the room is free in green. This way, you should not be disturbed in those lessons where you want to focus just on your class and pupils can plan for when they will use the ICT room, taking responsibility for their own work and time management.

Consider forming an ICT club at lunchtimes or after school to further students' enthusiasm and learning – see page 105 for more on extra-curricular activity ideas.

Activities done in free time

We all hope that pupils will work during their free time, whether on ICT or other subjects. You can encourage this by maintaining the atmosphere of a conventional classroom, allowing primacy to those students wanting to work and encouraging other teachers to set homework needing the use of ICT. However, you may wish to support other types of ICT use during lunchtimes or before or after school. If you have filtering software, it may switch on to a different mode at these times and allow access to more websites (such as video sites), social networking sites or online games. Alternatively, pupils could have a different log-on for these times, perhaps with the password changing every day and which they only find out once they go in during these times.

Even if pupils are just surfing the web or playing games, they are still developing ICT skills – do not think they are wasting their time, even if they think they are. It may be that you need to explain to other teachers in the school that giving them this time to 'chill out' and do something non-school related is enabling them to keep developing their skills without realizing it and also gives them time to reflect on their learning. Pupils need to work hard, but constantly bombarding them with information is like throwing mud at a wall – some of it will stick, some won't, but the more you throw, and the more covered the wall gets, the less will stick with each throw. Pupils need time to reflect on their learning, clear their minds and prepare themselves for the next lot of information they will receive.

Try to set up these free-time sessions so that pupils will be more easily able to do things which are educational, even though they don't realize it. Perhaps put shortcuts on the desktop, provide links from the VLE or put posters on the walls suggesting what they might like to do – 'If you're bored, try this . . .' These activities could include:

- **Surfing on the internet:** Rather than mindlessly surfing or looking at websites they normally look at, suggest other sites they might like or challenge them to find answers to questions which provide interesting factoids.
- **Chatting:** When pupils are using email, social networking sites and forums it may seem like they are just creating mindless banter about inane topics. In fact, they are improving their typing skills every time they enter a message and, to some extent, their English skills. Even if they are writing in online shorthand, they are still using language to communicate. It seems to some that using this online language is preventing them from developing skills in spelling; however, because they have to consider the words phonetically and as syllables, they are

probably thinking more about how to create words than they have done since they learned to read and write. Suggest good sites where they can chat about ideas, citizenship, interesting topics or perhaps a good foreign language site so they can practice their French, Spanish or whichever language they happen to be learning.

-   **Playing games:** Although large-scale, commercial games may not be allowed, small online games might be, and these can be put to good use. Consider not allowing access to all online games – just a selection. Make sure the selection is wide enough to cater to a wide range of tastes so pupils do not get bored, and alter the selection perhaps every term. You could offer games which are educational, such as those specifically designed for pupils learning a certain subject – these are especially good around the times when pupils are revising for exams. However, consider other games which can develop different skills. There are many touch-typing games available which also develop English skills as pupils are required to type words in with the correct spelling quickly. Games which involve puzzles can exercise English or Maths skills. Decision-making games, where the consequences of their choices have an effect on their character, often fit in well with PSHE topics. Also consider co-ordination and spatial-awareness games including classics such as *Tetris* and *Pong*, both of which develop more areas of the brain than most people realize, including hand–eye co-ordination, speed prediction, path direction and deflection, and logic. See this book's companion website for suggestions of games. You could set up an in-school competition that includes the whole school, just one year group or just those who are interested, including the staff. If the game is surreptitiously educational then it should get the backing from staff and be fun for pupils to practise in the hope of winning. The competition itself could be set up as an event, with a small group of spectators and each competitor paying an entry fee which could go to charity.

Leisure ICT at home

Just like in their free time at school, it can be beneficial for pupils to use ICT at home. They may do the same activities online as they do at school, although it is likely that they will have access to anything on the internet. Encourage teachers of other subjects to set homework involving ICT, bearing in mind that pupils will have different software and levels of access at home. If ICT is available to use at school, then pupils have no excuse for not doing it, even if they do not have a computer or internet at home, because they have had the opportunity to do it at school.

Pupils' use of ICT at home could be focused just like at school by teachers providing links to interesting sites and games, organizing competitions and challenges and encouraging use of 'safe', fascinating forums. As the internet is a living, breathing thing, be aware that no website which allows users to add content (such as on message boards or chatting) can ever be 'safe' as it can never be predicted what other people will say. It is advisable that when you suggest websites, games or links you provide a disclaimer stating that, although the school is recommending these sites, you cannot be held liable for the content. If pupils have good eSafety knowledge, they will hopefully be able to identify inappropriateness and know what to do if it occurs. See Chapter 5 for more information on eSafety.

At school we are able to closely monitor pupils as to which websites they go to and filter and block those which are unsuitable and restrict access. At home, however, it is a different matter. If it is possible for you to invite parents in for an eSafety workshop or send a letter home giving advice (without being patronizing) then it is a worthwhile exercise, as many parents are not aware of the dangers associated with the internet or what they could do about them. There is advice which can be given to pupils, but there is also other advice which can be given directly to parents/guardians. See Chapter 5 and this book's companion website for advice which can be printed for parents or emailed home as an attachment.

Extra-curricular activities

As well as encouraging the use of ICT by your pupils in their free time, you can provide extra-curricular activities which can encourage use of ICT and teach them skills you would otherwise not get the opportunity to teach them. Extra-curricular activities enrich a pupil's education and allow them to explore their interests. Although most involve learning new skills, because there is no pressure of exams or coursework there is freedom to experiment and the learning environment can be more relaxed. This can sometimes be the trigger that develops an interest in lifelong learning as it shows another dimension to education, one which is fun and stress-free. It is also a good opportunity to build strong relationships with the pupils involved and develop a committed team who can then promote the activity or subject throughout the school. In addition, it is a privilege which can be taken away if necessary if any pupils involved misbehave and one which they must earn again.

Lesson Activity: *Ideas for Extra-curricular ICT*

Extra-curricular ICT could take the form of a group which meets regularly. Students could do different tasks together, or the group could be set up to create a certain product.

Ideas for ICT extra-curricular activities include:

- **Create a podcast or vodcast** about the school, life at school, or a monthly 'newsletter' on events and activities or any other topic.
- **Create a school newspaper** which could be released regularly, fortnightly, monthly or termly. If a standard template is used, each year group could do it once a year, which would mean in a school with seven year groups it could be published once every half term (not including upper sixth as they should be busy preparing for A-levels or equivalents and life after school). It could be published in-school or, if done professionally, go out to parents/guardians. It could include what's hot and what's not (in pupils' opinions), current affairs, short stories, interviews with teachers, updates on performance in Sport, Drama, Music and other subjects, recipes and any other topics which might be of interest. Pupils could get involved in carrying out interviews, writing the pieces, formatting the newspaper, adding graphics and printing the final product, with each part of the process developing different sets of skills.
- **Work on the school website or VLE.** By giving the pupils an area on either of these systems, they can get involved in an active ICT system, just like in the real world, and this can also encourage use by other pupils. Pupils often learn better from other pupils and will be interested to see what content they add. This area could work like an online magazine or have blogs, forums or suggested links. It could be educational, with pupils setting up their own support network to discuss homework and coursework, or it could involve bigger issues such as life at school, advice or other forms of entertainment, such as discussing the latest cool television shows or fashions. The hard part about this for teachers is relinquishing input and responsibility. However, if you completely hand this area over to the pupils, give them the ownership and responsibility and show you trust them, you will be amazed at what they can produce – probably something better than you or I could come up with. However, even if you do give them complete control, always preview what they have created before it goes online. This should be done openly, explaining why you just need to give it a final seal of approval before it goes live to the whole school (or wider audience). They will understand and will appreciate your

honesty, and it is much better than you doing something underhand without their knowledge.

- **Make resources for other subjects** using animation, games design and other multimedia software. This gives pupils an opportunity to learn skills they may not cover in lessons and also put them to practical use, rather than just producing something for the sake of it. They will have to work to a tight brief given by the teacher of the other subject and work as a team. They will also have to invent an idea and make sure it is appropriate and educational and deliver the completed product on time. This provides a great replica of a real-world process and will give them an insight into how multimedia teams like this operate, perhaps sparking an interest in studying this field further. They will also feel pride in seeing their resource being used to teach other pupils in the school and, if the subject teacher credits them, it will give them a sense of satisfaction in a good job well done. It will also promote involvement in extra-curricular activity among other pupils.

- **Teach people in the community.** You could set up a scheme where people from the community come into the school for a 30-minute session each week and your students teach them how to use ICT. This would forge excellent links with the community and also benefit your students, as sometimes the best way to learn something is by showing someone else. The people you could advertise it to would be those who were available to come into the school during the day, including people who are retired, stay-at-home parents and the unemployed. Obviously you need to be present at these sessions and supervise them carefully, making sure the people from outside are suitable and the students are doing a good job. The adults could be evaluated by those they have been teaching, perhaps at the end of each term, and those with the highest scores could win a prize. Also there are external awards available for pupils who teach ICT to people outside their school.

- **Mentoring other pupils.** More experienced and able pupils could mentor younger or weaker pupils in using ICT. It could be quite specific mentoring, in that the mentors teach the mentees skills they have been trying to develop in class, or it could be extra skills which they have not covered in class, perhaps with the aim of producing something together, such as a short animation. Although this would be good for high-achieving pupils, it would mostly benefit pupils who are average because if they see they can show other pupils who are weaker than them how to use ICT, it will bolster their confidence and perhaps improve their own skills at the same time.

5

eSafety: The Skills to Be Safe Online

You will see a lot of books and articles about eSafety that start by saying something like, 'Communication technology is becoming increasingly widespread and accessible, not just at home and in school but also on the move.' But you don't need this spelling out to you, because you already know that technology is not just increasing – it's everywhere, it's pervasive. It's not just growing – it's *here*. We know this, we see it every day. It's something we have had to deal with for a while, even before legislation, school policy and popular chat shows caught up with what was actually happening in the classroom.

In a recent study by Beatbullying the following results were found from surveying over 2,000 young people:

- One in three 11–16-year-olds has been cyberbullied.
- One in thirteen of this age group have been persistently, systematically cyberbullied in a prolonged campaign.
- Cyberbullying is becoming multi-faceted and cross-platform; what may start out on instant messenger may then progress to social networking, mobile phones, etc.
- One-third of this age group had received a 'sext', a text containing words or images of a sexual nature.
- Only 2 per cent of 'sexts' were sent by adults.
- There have been 16 suicides officially attributed to cyberbullying in the UK – it is thought there have actually been more.

This is a serious issue which needs to be dealt with by sharing information, awareness and protection by teachers and parents – and the pupils themselves.

This chapter will discuss the three main areas of eSafety which cause issues with young people, with the aim of providing information and highlighting key areas of which you should be knowledgeable and attentive to. Ideas to educate your pupils and strategies for continued monitoring and support of your message are also discussed.

Young people have mobile phones – in fact, just about everyone has one – and these phones have remarkable capabilities which provide access, freedom and opportunities for communication. They are fantastic tools, especially for those who are isolated or need help. Parents and children can stay in contact and the phones provide great reassurance for both; some mobiles even have GPS trackers so parents can literally watch a map and see where their child is. Mobile phones have not removed all the difficulties of keeping in touch and knowing where young people are, as there is still the problem of making sure it is charged, turned on and has credit, but these difficulties are reducing as technology improves.

Keeping in touch with friends is a key use of ICT by young people. It has become enabling and empowering – and has mostly stopped them running up massive phone bills! Email, instant messaging, forums and social networking sites all facilitate communication, and those pupils who may feel lonely or separated from the mainstream can become whatever they want online, develop their own character or appear under a pseudonym. It can be a tool which builds confidence, which allows students to experience socializing and learn the rules of engagement. It can also can help them overcome shyness or introversion.

Online gaming is a hugely popular area of technology, whether it takes place on a console or PC. All major games are now released with online capabilities. From being able to share images or videos of their gameplay with each other to being able to talk in real time, live with other players, the online experience is as important as the offline one. Some games are purely online, with Massively Multiplayer Online games (MMOs) existing purely in a shared online world. Playing online means that game playing is no longer a solitary activity, but one which involves communication, teamwork and interaction with other human beings.

If the internet was turned off tomorrow, if all the web servers suddenly stopped working, life as we know it would grind to a halt. No matter how much you might think you wouldn't be affected, we are all dependent on it to differing degrees; it is an integral part of our civilization. As such, our young people should have access to the internet and use it to its full potential. If you block them from using it, not only are you preventing them from learning about one of the most important tools they will need to understand for their futures but also, kids being kids, they will find a way around your blocks. Using tools to limit what young people can see and preventing them from being exposed to the nasty parts of the internet is our duty, and it is right to prohibit use of distracting sites, such as games and social networking, during lessons. However, using these protective tools to block access to parts of the internet will not only frustrate your pupils (and make them determined to find a way around your system), it will also prevent you from delivering important lessons about online safety and the importance of being open about what they do online.

> ⊶ If you force your pupils to keep their online activities secret, if you make it something wrong and illicit, they will only want to do it more, and when they do have problems they will be less likely to come to you for help.
>
> By keeping an open line of communication about what they do online, we can provide students with advice and support, without having to lecture them or teach them everything in a formal lesson. We hope that parents communicate with their children and provide an environment where they can discuss anything and ask for help – we must do the same, especially if that is not happening at home.
>
> In addition, when online we must be good role models and show good practice at all times. We cannot tell pupils not to put up embarrassing pictures of themselves then do so ourselves!

We all know there are risks associated with the internet; however, to play a full part in our modern society, to be true digital citizens and to be genuinely prepared for their lives in the future, they should not be prevented from developing the skills they will need online. Rather than restricting their use, we need to focus on educating them and making them safe, informed users.

eSafety should be approached as a large-scale campaign, with all pupils and staff on board and with needs continually reinforced. In some schools, senior management may choose to lead on this issue, in others it may fall under the remit of the ICT department. Your school should have an eSafety policy, or, better, one policy for pupils and one for staff, as the approach to each and rules to be followed can be quite dissimilar. In addition, you should also have an Acceptable Use Policy (AUP) which is an agreement between each user, pupils and staff, and the school, who owns the network. This will explicitly state what is acceptable and what is not. It not only highlights your school's ICT rules, but also declares the terms by which users might be punished for misuse. For example, if a pupil uses a school computer to search for pornography, action can be taken if the AUP states they cannot use the school computers for this purpose. It removes any argument which may occur – and if the pupil has signed the AUP, they cannot deny being aware of the rules.

eSafety is a crucial part of the Every Child Matters agenda, which contains five key principles:

- being healthy
- staying safe
- enjoying and achieving
- making a positive contribution
- achieving economic well-being.

The aim is for agencies to work together to provide a better service for young people and to give each the best possible start in life.

> It is important to remember, and to remind pupils (and staff), that future admissions officers and employers do look at a person's online profiles as part of the application procedure, whether it be a simple web search or specifically looking for their social networking profile. If your pupils have aspirations of going to university or getting a job at any time in the future, they need to be very careful of what they have put online. I do know of a real case where a pupil was turned down for university due to the pictures on her Facebook profile. With competition for places and jobs being so high, there has to be some way of shortening the list of applicants – finding something inappropriate about them online is a simple way of doing this. Once something is put online, it can never fully be removed – there will always be a trace of it somewhere.

The Child Exploitation and Online Protection Centre (CEOP) is the lead organization in the UK for eSafety, and a branch of law enforcement. Their work is truly making a difference. If you have the opportunity to attend their training sessions or conferences, I would strongly advise attending. Visit their website at www.ceop.gov.uk and www.thinkuknow.co.uk for more information about CEOP and the information they have available. By becoming a CEOP Ambassador you gain access to fantastic materials which make the delivery of the eSafety message a lot easier – more hard-hitting and more memorable.

Although this section is focused on pupils, staff can also be at risk online and need to be informed and aware of the issues, partly as a component of their duty of care, partly to protect themselves. There have been incidents of teachers being filmed in class and the result being posted online; staff putting too much personal information about themselves online and pupils finding it; and teachers becoming online 'friends' with pupils. This leads to some very blurred lines inside and out of school and teachers putting themselves in compromising positions, even if nothing inappropriate has occurred.

Cyberbullying

As we all know, bullying is nasty, cowardly and cruel, but is something which exists and is very difficult to deal with. The range of methods available to the bully is quite wide: physical, emotional, psychological, social exclusion, etc. With the development of technology, a new avenue has arisen: cyberbullying, which is the use of any technology to deliberately upset someone else. This includes the use of both computers and mobile phones.

Examples can include:

- **Setting up a website or group about the victim.** Websites can be set up easily and with no cost. There are a number of free hosting services where anyone can have a website they have created uploaded to the internet and which can be seen by anyone. Web design is taught in schools as part of an ICT curriculum, usually beginning at ages 11–13 but sometimes also in primary schools. Groups can be instigated within social networking websites with ease and the owner of the group can decide whether it can be seen by anyone or a select group of users.
- **Filming others and posting on the internet.** Most modern mobile phones have capabilities for taking digital photographs and recording sound and video footage. Whereas these used to have grainy, indistinct audio and visual quality, they are improving rapidly and beginning to reach the quality of camcorders. Recording on a mobile phone can look like normal phone usage and lights and sounds which usually indicate that photographs or video are being taken can be disabled, meaning there can be no warning that it is taking place. In addition, most modern laptops have webcams and microphones built in, which

can be used to record sound and images. Incidents also include 'happy slapping', where a fight is filmed then shared between mobiles or posted on the internet. The victims of happy slapping are usually unsuspecting members of the public who are set upon by several attackers. The severity of attacks ranges widely, but some have resulted in permanent injury and death. Happy slapping appears to be losing popularity, but still occurs periodically.

- **Sending insulting and vicious text messages.** All modern mobile phones are capable of sending text messages and a high proportion of these can also perform multimedia messaging where photographs, audio clips and video clips can be sent and received. In addition, there are several internet sites which allow a user to send anonymous text messages for free.
- **Posting fake and obscene photographs of the victim.** An increasing number of young people have access at school and at home to high-quality image manipulation software such as Adobe Photoshop or Corel PaintShop Pro, which can produce professional-quality images. In addition there are numerous free packages available from the internet such as Picasa from Google and GIMP. A typical image created is the victim's head on the body of someone naked or overweight.
- **Circulating material from a personal or social networking site.** Users of social networking sites (such as Facebook, MySpace, LinkedIn, Twitter) can post photographs of themselves, enabling other users to save a copy. This could then be spread (either as is or edited) by others on the social networking site or by email, multimedia text message or instant messaging (such as MSN Messenger).

Adults are also at risk of being cyberbullied, and there have been cases of it happening in the workplace. Therefore teachers can be exposed to it, from pupils or other teachers. It is an area which should not be overlooked, especially when pupils can use the internet to victimize certain teachers, thinking they do not know enough about the internet to find it or do anything about it. The more informed and aware your staff are, the better protected your whole school will be.

Bullying vs. cyberbullying

Physical, mental and emotional forms of traditional bullying are serious issues for young people and on the whole are being dealt with proactively by schools and organizations working with young people. Cyberbullying has mostly the same features as bullying, but with some additional challenging characteristics:

- **Invasion of personal space.** With traditional bullying, the bullies generally have to be in close proximity to their victim, whereas cyberbullies can reach their victim anywhere. The mobile phone carried in their pocket and the computer in their bedroom become weapons to continue the threats and taunts even when the victim is in their own home. Moving to another school, which is sometimes used in serious prolonged cases of bullying, is no longer an option as the victim can be contacted anywhere at any time.
- **Anonymity of the bully.** Cyberbullies can hide behind anonymity or a fake identity on the internet. Accordingly, the victim does not know who is perpetrating the bullying and the bully is given the confidence to go further. What they may never say in person is easier to type or text if they think their identity cannot be discovered.
- **Speed of transmission of messages or images.** Emails, posts on the internet and text messages are instantaneous. Messages or images can be sent without the sender taking time to reconsider. Although it may be a case of 'cyberbully in haste, repent at leisure', once the send button has been pressed or clicked, it cannot be taken back.
- **Those who would not normally take part in traditional bullying may pass on images received by mobile or email.** Cyberbullying attracts people who would not usually become involved in bullying. The anonymity of it can give a false sense of power and the effect on the victim is not seen when the cyberbullying happens. A vicious text message about a victim may be sent to someone not previously involved in bullying, but if they forward it to others they are now part of it.

There is one positive feature of cyberbullying, compared with face-to-face bullying, which is that the evidence can be preserved. Unlike the 'he said she said' nature of traditional bullying, cyberbullying involves the digital written word, images which can be copied and videos which can be saved. Proof of what has been said or shown can be used as confirmation of events and to find the perpetrators.

The effects of bullying

I've heard it said that bullying is just 'a part of growing up', that it is inevitable and can be seen as positive because it makes young people stronger, or that schools are powerless to act, especially if it is going on outside of school.

This is nonsense.

Bullying should never be a part of a person's life and, if it is, all possible steps should be taken to eradicate it. Not only should every child have a safe environment in which to learn and grow but they should also have a route to take to find help and support when needed.

In 2006 Megan Meier was an average 13-year-old girl, doing what 13-year-old girls do. She enjoyed chatting with her friends on MySpace and one day made 'friends' with a boy calling himself 'Josh Evans'. They became very close, talking online daily. The conversations, however, turned and became nasty and threatening. Tragically things got so out of hand that Megan ended up committing suicide. Only afterwards was it discovered that the boy wasn't a boy at all and was actually the mother of a friend of Megan's with whom she'd had a falling out.

Sadly Megan is not the only young person to have taken their own life as a result of cyberbullying. This is why it is so important for you to be aware of it and to be armed with strategies to keep you and your students safe.

Privacy

Privacy is an issue many pupils have difficulty understanding. They see no problem with putting their personal details online, or their innermost thoughts and dreams or even photographs of themselves or others. 'What's wrong with that?' is what I'm most often asked. It's only when I explain the consequences of posting details like this that they begin to realize how it could get them into difficult situations and even danger. Who might be looking at that picture? What might they be thinking when they look at it? Might they have saved a copy? Who else might they have passed it to?

Email is ubiquitous and something we don't think twice about now. Whereas even into the early years of the noughties we would ask, 'Do you have an email address?', it is now just assumed everyone has one, possibly more than one. It is important to remember that once that send button has been clicked, those words you have written are no longer under your control. Even though it is digital, it is still the written word and pupils should be reminded that if they would not say it to someone's face, or write it in a letter, they should not email it. All emails can be saved, printed or forwarded to other people. If Jared sends an email to Zulfiker saying something nasty about Izzy, it is perfectly possible for Zulfiker to forward that email to Izzy, or Izzy's parents, or Izzy's tutor or even the head. Therefore, pupils should be reminded that they need to be very careful about what they say in their emails.

> ⟜ Staff should also be careful about the content of their emails. It is good advice that if you need to send an email of complaint, write it and then sleep on it so you can have another look at it in the morning when you've calmed down, because once you've sent it you can't take it back. How many times have you said something and then wished you could take it back – with an email you can give yourself that time to consider whether it should be sent, or whether it should be reworded or not sent at all. Also, be aware that some schools monitor teachers' online activity when they are using school-owned computers and laptops or are on the school network. This could include the websites you visit and the emails you send. It is always useful to familiarize yourself with the school's ICT policies.
>
> Schools face another issue as well: documentation can be requested from the school about a particular pupil under the Freedom of Information Act 2000. This could include any emails which have been sent about them between teachers. Be very careful about what you put in writing about any pupil, no matter how much they've irritated you that day.

Social networking sites, instant messaging and forums can sometimes provide the perfect place for personal details to be revealed and some users' whole purpose is to extract those details, possibly for grooming (see page 125) or identity theft.

The following advice, which is also included on this book's companion website as a printable handout or poster, could be given to pupils about personal information:

- Use a pseudonym rather than your real name.
- NEVER give out personal information, either in your profile or in any messages you post. Never give out your home address, phone numbers or email addresses.

- Before posting any messages, consider what you are saying. Never feel pressured to give out information about yourself, either personal details or private thoughts and feelings.
- Think very carefully before posting any pictures. You should not put pictures of yourself or anyone else on the internet, especially embarrassing ones. Once you have posted them you will never know who has a copy. Keep those holiday snaps of you in shorts or bikinis away from the internet.
- Do not put anything in your profile that you would not tell a stranger on the street. Have a profile that you would be happy for your parents/ guardians or the head to see.
- Remember that university admissions tutors and future employers are now looking at social networking sites as part of the selection process.

The following advice, which is also included on this book's companion website as a printable handout or poster, could be given to pupils about forums, instant messaging and social networking sites:

- Make sure your profile is set to a high level of privacy and check carefully what information can be viewed by other users (such as personal information, contact details and messages you post).
- Do not make your friends list available to others; your friends may not be very happy if strangers can see them.
- Do not agree to be friends with people you have never met. You can never be sure who they really are.
- Think carefully before joining any groups, especially if your messages can be read by anybody.
- You should not join any groups which are offensive to an individual or a group of people (these break Facebook's own rules and you could be banned from using their site).
- You should not join any spoof or fake groups (e.g. for a school or a person) as these are potentially libellous and anyone involved risks prosecution.
- If you are not happy with a group, leave it. This avoids you being involved in any investigation and subsequent sanctions by Facebook or the school if the group is found to be in breach of their rules.
- Remember that your profile may still be seen by others, even with privacy settings turned on, through a friend network (e.g. you are friends with Tanya; Tanya is friends with Brian; therefore Brian can see your profile).
- Remember anything you put online, even if you later remove it, might

already have been copied by someone else. Any messages you post or pictures you upload are no longer your property.

The key message is that if a pupil is not happy about anything that is happening online they need to keep the evidence, withdraw from the conversation and log off the site, and tell someone straight away.

The 3 P's: Prowlers, predators and paedophiles

Prowlers, predators and paedophiles are those people who will prey on children for their own gain. They will exploit them for personal pleasure and distribute images for illegal gain. The introduction of and broadening access to the internet benefits society in innumerable positive ways; however, it has also opened up new opportunities for those looking to abuse children. Young people and adults should be aware of this issue and know what to do if they encounter it.

Adults who wish to sexually abuse children will sometimes 'groom' them first, deliberately befriending them and establishing a relationship of trust. It will often begin with establishing a friendship, perhaps based on a common interest. The adult may take on a persona that is a similar age to the person they are chatting with – remember, online you can never be sure whom you are talking to.

This friendship generally begins to develop via positive reinforcement and making the child feel special. Sometimes it will involve turning them against established relationships, breaking the bond and establishing a stronger bond with the adult, so it seems they are the only one who the child can depend on. For example:

Child: Everyone thinks I'm ugly.
Adult: Not me. I think you're gorgeous.

Child: It's so unfair my parents won't let me go to Mike's party.
Adult: They're stupid. You should be able to go.

If the adult has been contacting the child through public areas they may then encourage the child to chat with them one-to-one in private. As part of the grooming process, they may talk about issues normally discussed between adults, such as marital problems, or topics of a sexual nature. The child may feel trusted and proud to be thought of as mature enough to be able to deal with these issues. They might give the child gifts, whether online or items in real life. They may show the child images or videos of pornography, introducing the idea or attempting to normalize such activities. This may then lead to the child being encouraged to send pictures of themselves or show themselves on their webcam. The nature of the requests may increase and can lead to organizing a meeting. The whole process of grooming is an escalation with an aim in mind, whether it be to obtain images or video, or to meet the child.

In 2009 the body of Ashleigh Hall, a 17-year-old girl from Darlington, was found abandoned in a ditch on farmland. She had told her mother she was going to stay overnight at a friend's house, but instead she had arranged to meet a 16-year-old boy she had been chatting with on Facebook. That 'boy' turned out to be a 32-year-old registered sex offender who proceeded to kidnap and murder her.

There are steps which can be taken to prevent this sort of tragedy, to protect our young people and to make them more aware:

- ensure students understand why they should keep their personal information private and what details they should not give out online
- help them understand that people may not tell the truth online or be the person they say they are
- keep the lines of communication open so they can talk about what they do online
- be familiar with the terminology of the internet
- monitor the websites being accessed
- make sure they know what to do if they do encounter something which makes them feel uncomfortable online.

There are additional steps which parents can take:

- discuss with their children what they are doing online
- check their child's browsing history
- have the computer with internet access used only in a family area rather than in the child's bedroom
- set realistic rules for use and stick to them; establish that if the screen changes or goes blank when someone walks past there could be sanctions
- check mobile phones as well – this should be done as a last resort, as the young person may see it as an invasion of their privacy.

If a child does feel uncomfortable online, they should tell someone. This could be a friend or a family member or it may be a member of school staff whom they trust. Don't expect them to use the 'proper' channels of speaking to their tutor or someone else with pastoral care responsibility; it may be simply a teacher they feel they can talk to. If a pupil does speak to you about an issue online, or wishes to report abuse, there are guidelines which you can follow. The following are the basic steps that teaching staff are advised to follow in the event that a child wishes to confide in a teacher that he or she is likely to be at risk.

- Create a safe environment for the child by taking the child to a private area within the school.
- Stay calm and listen carefully to what the child has to say, taking what the child has to say seriously. If the child starts to confide in you about a potentially abusive situation, acknowledge that it may be difficult for the child.
- If the child does report a child protection concern, reassure the child that he/she is not to blame but do not promise confidentiality.
- Be honest with the child and do not make promises you cannot keep. In particular, explain that you will have to tell other people in order to help them and explain that you will not be able to keep it a secret.
- Try to be clear about what the child is saying to you and keep questions to a minimum, avoiding closed questions. Allow the child to use his/her own words and avoid the child having to repeat what they are telling you.
- Remember that an allegation of child abuse may lead to a criminal conviction. Consequently, avoid doing anything that may jeopardize a police investigation such as asking leading questions. Once the initial concerns have been reported to you, discuss your concerns with the designated Child Protection Officer in your school or the head teacher.
- The designated Child Protection Officer within your school should immediately refer the matter to the Children's Social Care Department in line with the locally agreed interagency child protection procedures. While teachers should seek, in general, to discuss any concerns with the child's family and where possible, seek their agreement to make the referral to the LA Children's Social Care, this should only be done where such discussion and agreement-seeking will not place a child at increased risk of significant harm. Sharing of information in cases of concern about children's welfare enables professionals to consider jointly how to proceed in the best interests of the child and to safeguard children more generally.
- When making the referral to Children's Social Care, you can expect the recipient of the referral to clarify with you the nature of the concern,

how it has arisen, what action you should take next and particularly what the child and the parents will be told, by whom and when.

- You will be required to make a written record of what the child reported to you and your responses. This must be done as soon as practicably possible and within 12 hours.
- If you are referring an alleged incident of contemporary abuse to the Children's Social Care, it is likely that the matter will immediately be referred on to the police and an initial strategy discussion will ensue. The strategy meeting will decide whether to initiate enquiries under s47 of the Children Act 1989 and therefore to commence a core assessment. It will also consider the necessity for emergency protective action to protect the child.
- Dealing with child protection matters can be stressful and emotionally demanding. Teaching staff are encouraged to seek support from line managers and occupational health support staff.

(Reproduced with kind permission from the Child Exploitation and Online Protection (CEOP) Centre.)

If a child does not feel they can speak to anyone about the incident, there is an alternative way of reporting online activity which makes them feel uncomfortable. The website www.thinkuknow.co.uk has been set up by CEOP, with support from the UK Council for Child Internet Safety (UKCCIS), the European Commission and law enforcement agencies, to provide advice and protection to young people online. If young people experience something online which makes them feel uncomfortable, they can use the 'CEOP Report' button on this website. This will then ask them to report what has happened. This report is sent directly to CEOP and the young person may be contacted by a member of social services or the police. By reporting their experiences, even if the young person may think it is minor, they are protecting themselves, their friends and young people all over the world. The 'CEOP Report' button is also available on other websites, and there is a call for it to be included on all websites which young people frequent.

How can you spread the eSafety message?

Information and awareness are key in protecting young people online. The more they know about the risks and what can be done, the more they are empowered and in control of their online experience. eSafety is not about preventing young people from using the internet and mobile phones – quite the opposite. It is about encouraging use, but making sure students know how to do it safely. Simple steps like not giving out personal details, not talking to strangers and staying on recognized websites can significantly reduce the risk to which they are exposed.

The message of eSafety needs to be conveyed to all young people, all education staff and as many parents as possible. Unfortunately it does have a reputation for being a boring and dry subject, and considered to be all about rules and regulations. Therefore, if you are delivering lessons, workshops or events on eSafety you need to quickly smash that stereotype and ensure your audience are involved and interested, as this is one of the most important subjects you can teach. The information you are sharing could be the difference between your pupils being safe and putting themselves in danger. It deserves time and effort and to be an issue of importance throughout your school.

How can I find out what's going on?

You can never be fully aware of everything that is going on with every pupil, especially in very large schools. However, you can take steps to gather as much information as possible.

Ask them

A straightforward way of doing this is by running a survey. If answers are entirely anonymous, pupils will feel much more inclined to be honest in their answers; you are not trying to find out who is doing what, but instead to get an overall picture. The survey could be on paper, and you could place a locked box somewhere, perhaps in reception, for pupils to post their completed answers. Alternatively, it could be online, perhaps using your VLE, although you will need to reassure pupils that you will be reliable and honest in your pledge for anonymity and will not trace back who has submitted which answers.

The questions need to be as simple as possible, both in terms of understanding and answering – tick boxes would suffice (see this book's companion website for a downloadable and editable example). Filling it in should not be seen as a chore or another piece of work, although you could leave space on the back, or a box at the bottom, for any longer comments the pupil wishes to make. You are never going to get a 100 per cent return rate from this survey, but you should get enough responses to obtain meaningful results.

Once the deadline for the submission of all questionnaires has passed, analyse the results. Make sure the pupils see the results from the survey, even if they are not as positive as you hoped. By sharing the results, pupils will feel part of the process of eSafety, will be more positive towards any changes which need to be made and be more inclined to take part in future surveys.

If the results are good, then you still need to keep reinforcing the eSafety message. If they are not so good, then more needs to be done and there needs to be a whole-school strategy on how that might be tackled.

Take more surveys, perhaps once a year, or before and after your eSafety campaign, that will hopefully show improvement. By gathering this data you will be able to be more aware of what is happening in your school. You will also have empirical data rather than guesswork and hearsay.

Check them

You could provide an online profile-checking service where pupils could ask you to check their social networking profiles.

> ☍ In order for them to use your online profile-checking service, you will need to give it a cool name, such as 'iSafe'. It's amazing the difference giving something a funky name can have!

Students would need to submit to you their full name, their online name and which sites they are registered on (e.g. Facebook, MySpace, Xbox LIVE, etc.). You can then do a thorough search for factors such as how meticulously they have set their privacy settings, how visible they are and whether their profile image is appropriate. See this book's companion website for helpsheets for changing security settings on social networking profiles.

You could even set it up as a rewards scheme – each pupil who has their profile checked could be allowed to use social networking sites in school at lunchtimes, for example.

Once they have submitted their profiles to be checked, part of the process could be that it is checked regularly, perhaps every couple of weeks or couple of months, to ensure it is all still OK. This could become quite burdensome for the person in charge of ICT as more and more pupils sign up, so perhaps the tutors in the school could become involved. If they are shown how to check their tutees' profiles, they could perhaps do a check once a month.

Search for them

There will always be pupils who put messages, images or videos onto the internet that they shouldn't, either naively or knowingly. Even if you are doing transparent checking of pupils' online activities, it is also advisable to do regular checks of online activities without specifying when and what you will be searching for. Hopefully, if you advertise the fact that you are doing these random checks this should be enough to deter most pupils from putting up anything they know is a bad idea; however, there will always be some who still do.

The best way to start this sort of search is to type in the name of your school in a search engine, video sharing site or social networking site. Also try typing in names of pupils who might be likely candidates. I appreciate that it is improper to single out pupils and suspect them of wrongdoing without evidence, but realistically there will be pupils whom you know are more likely than others to do things – and if you don't find anything under their names that is a positive thing that you can then draw upon in your dealings with those pupils. The pupils you might wish to try searching for are those who are prone to misbehaving, those who are very ICT literate, those who spend a lot of time online and also those who may not run with the 'popular crowds' in the school and can seem isolated. It is not possible to search for all pupils; therefore, targeting some of them is the best you can do. You may wish to search for pupils' names at random. Ensure you check for each year group; being older or younger does not make them any more or less likely to be involved in eSafety issues.

When searching online, you are looking for and may find all sorts of materials. These might include unsecure social networking profiles, spoof websites about pupils or staff, defamatory materials about the school or videos of pupils or staff. When doing this, you need to ensure that your senior management are aware of your searches. If you do find anything, you need to be clear about your school policy of the steps to be taken. Do you deal with the pupil directly or is the matter passed up to senior management? Also be aware that you may find materials which demonstrate a pupil is at risk and you may need to follow your school's child protection policy and take action immediately. It is important if you do find anything to gather evidence by recording the date of discovery and documenting your actions taken to find it (to demonstrate you found it without 'hacking').

School bullying policy

Your school policy on bullying should include a section specifically on cyberbullying. It should be clear about what action can and should be taken in the event of suspicion or disclosure of cyberbullying. For example, in your AUP you may have a section that declares that the school, as owners of the network, are able to look at all materials stored on it, including emails and files. The best weapon we have against cyberbullying is physical evidence, the trail it leaves, the screenshots which can be taken, the text messages which can be saved, etc.

A key element of school policy is making all pupils aware. If they are informed, they are empowered. If potential bullies know that action will definitely be taken when they are found out, if they know you are actively alert for signs of bullying, if they know that they are not as anonymous online as they think they are, it will prevent some cyberbullying from happening. For those who still go ahead, their victims need to know where they can find help and how to collect proof – and that the school will do everything it can to protect them and stop the bullies.

School policy can be dry and boring – communicating it should not be. It needs to be clear, concise and interesting; the message needs to be heard and understood by all. If you have posters made by students, other students will pay more attention to them. Peer learning is often the most effective way to get a message across. In addition, although the staff and pupils are the primary responsibility, it is also important to inform parents and keep them aware of eSafety issues – what the school is doing to protect their children and how they can also help. This could range from a leaflet being posted to all parents – one which will grab their attention and persuade them to read it – to holding parental workshops or discussions forums (see page 134).

The following useful advice, which is also included on this book's companion website as a printable handout, can be given directly to parents/guardians:

- Consider the location of your home computer. If it is in a busy area of the house, you are able to keep an eye on what your child is doing online.
- Learn about the world your child is part of, including the acronyms and slang terms which are used. Get to know how the sites work and what to do if there is a problem, such as contacting the administrator or reporting an incident.
- Set up social networking, chat and email accounts on the same sites

as your child. Know their screen name(s) and make sure they are not including any personal information in their profiles.

- Regularly go through your child's 'friends' or 'buddies' with them. Ask your child who they are and how they know them. Discourage them from having 'friends' they have not met in real life.
- Talk to your child about cyberbullying, just as you might talk to your child about traditional bullying. Ask if they have ever seen it happen and what they should do about it if they see it again or it happens to them.
- Keep the line of communication open and tell your child that you won't take away their computer access if they disclose they are being cyberbullied (which is one of the main reasons why young people do not admit to it happening).

eSafety workshops

Workshops, as opposed to lessons, could be delivered to larger groups of pupils. I have used the term 'workshop' because I want to avoid the words 'lecture', 'presentation', 'talk' and other names which sound boring and will turn pupils off before they even arrive. You could alternatively use 'demonstration', 'session' or even 'conference' – any word which will show that this is not a normal event.

Workshops for pupils

Your workshops for pupils should be carefully considered as obviously the content for each needs to be slightly different, although the key messages remain the same. For pupils, it is about keeping themselves safe. You need to make sure your workshop is targeted at the appropriate age group and you may wish to deliver it to separate groups, perhaps each year group or lower school (Years 7 and 8) and upper school (Years 9 to 11), and deliver it to the sixth form separately, if you have one. Different issues will affect pupils of different ages. Younger pupils may feel more inclined to contribute and ask questions if the intimidating older years are not there; similarly older years may feel more confident asking about more mature topics if the younger pupils are not there. I once witnessed a sex-education-style presentation given to both Year 8 and Year 10 pupils at the same time which was highly unsuccessful. The presenter was restricted by the topics they could and couldn't cover in front of the younger pupils, describing the parts of the body in a simplified way, which was fine for the younger pupils but frustrating for the older ones. The older pupils, who were really interested and wanted to find out more, found their intricate questions could not be answered. Therefore, really consider what is best for your pupils.

Workshops for colleagues, parents and guardians

For presenting to staff and parents/guardians the focus is on keeping their pupils or children safe. For staff you should also include any relevant legislation, Every Child Matters, and their responsibilities under duty of care and *in loco parentis*. Also incorporate the risks to staff, including staff being filmed by pupils and those films being put on the internet; becoming 'friends' with pupils on social networking sites and putting up their personal details or images which pupils can access. Remember some pupils are very tech savvy. For parents/guardians, the focus needs to be on how they can protect their child/children at home. Consider that families will have different ICT capabilities at home, although you can assume that most will have a computer and some form of connection to the internet. Acknowledge that you cannot tell parents/guardians how to run their households, but you can make them aware of the issues and offer guidance.

Think about the last time you experienced a presentation which lasted at least an hour and required you to sit for the whole time. It may have been a lecture, conference or training session. Was it boring? Was it mostly someone talking at you, perhaps with a sedentary PowerPoint behind them? It is surprising how common these are. If we stood at the front each lesson and lectured to our pupils, not only would they be bored rigid but if we were being inspected by our senior management or Ofsted they would be very displeased. And yet, it seems to be acceptable to subject adults to this style of teaching. There has been a lot of research carried out to discover how long pupils can concentrate and the consensus for teenagers is about 20 minutes (shorter for younger pupils). We should, therefore, break our lessons into separate activities with ebb and flow to maintain momentum and interest. If you are delivering your workshop to adults, do not let all your teacher training disappear, but use it to create something vibrant and exciting. Adults are not able to sit still for an hour and digest all of the information that is told to them in that time if it is monotonous – we are just too polite to say anything! Teachers, who will likely be thinking about how much other work they have to do and will only be interested in what you have to say if it directly relates to their teaching, tend to have especially short attention spans. Think of any presentation like a lesson – if you would not talk for 20 minutes on one topic, then don't do it in your presentation. Keep it simple, short, interesting and, above all, relevant.

Adding an element of interactivity to the workshop is a great way to keep your audience interested. Below are a few ideas of how to do this:

- Give all or some of your audience red cards and whistles and ask them to be referees. Purposefully include incorrect information and ask your referees to blow their whistles and give it the red card when they think they have seen or heard it. This will not only keep them awake (via the regular loud toots on whistles) but will also make them focus on the pieces of information that they have spotted to be incorrect. If you have these as key points, when you give the correct information those chunks of information will be better remembered.
- Start by promising a surprise later on in the workshop; for example, 'Later in this workshop you will see a YouTube video of a pupil doing something naughty in school which they have filmed and put up online – stick around to find out who it was and what they did!'
- Ask for audience participation – it could be a showing of hands, chanting a phrase or answering a question. It could even be a rhetorical question that you ask them to ponder without giving the answer.
- Invite questions or comments from the audience. This needs to be managed carefully, as questions throughout the workshop can break the flow of delivery and can also divert the focus of the workshop, going off on a tangent. You could divide your workshop into short chunks and after each invite questions about that topic.
- Ask for a volunteer and invite them to the front to be involved in a task. You may ask them to write something on a flipchart or hold something up. If you are confident, you could involve them in a magic trick. Never embarrass your volunteer or ask them to relay personal experiences, and make sure they get a round of applause as they join you at the front and return to their seat.

Continuing with the theme of keeping your audience interested, it makes for a more interesting presentation if several methods of delivery are used, although make sure you don't flit around too much between delivery styles and lose your point. Remember, delivering the content and making sure it is remembered are the most important elements. Using multimedia is very effective, especially for young people, for whom experiencing several multimedia techniques in a short space of time is normal, and will also focus their attention. If you are an ICT teacher, use this as an opportunity to also demonstrate how ICT can make a presentation more powerful and memorable. Use video clips, audio clips, music, animation and other elements to keep it interesting.

Make sure you practise the workshop and set up any equipment well in advance. This may seem obvious but if you are nervous about delivering your workshop to a large audience and have a lot of other things on the go at the same time, it is easy to omit the most obvious parts. Practise all the way through so that when you actually deliver it, it is slick and there are no errors. Check for spelling and grammar mistakes in any materials you use (presentations or printouts). Make sure all your equipment works – test sound and video, check volume levels at the back of the room and test to make sure your lighting is suitable (and doesn't wash out your projection screen).

eSafety events

An eSafety event is something which would be bigger than a workshop, likely to be a whole day or week and involve several activities. This would need to be agreed to by your senior management team and it would help if you had the co-operation of the other staff in your school.

An eSafety day or week could comprise several activities and could include an afternoon or day off-timetable where the main part of the event occurs (or perhaps each year group has a different off-timetable period). Activities could include:

- making an eSafety short film or podcast (to be shown at the end of the event or in an assembly) – this could be run as a competition
- a quiz about eSafety:
  ~ pupils could search the school for the questions and then provide the answers on worksheets (they would need to know how many questions there are)
  ~ a *Who Wants to Be a Millionaire*-style quiz with the other pupils as audience
  ~ a *University Challenge*-style quiz with the other pupils as audience.
- inviting guest speakers to talk about eSafety
- visiting other schools or inviting their pupils to your school to talk about eSafety
- inviting parents/guardians and local residents to your school to be involved in the event.

In conclusion, here are some dates for your diary:

- Safer Internet Day – run every year in February
- Anti-bullying Week – run every year in November.

Join the national and international campaigns to protect all young people online.

6

Taking ICT Further: Imagination, Independence and Inspiration

ICT may sometimes be seen as a 'geeky' subject, suitable for those people who like maths and electronics and programming, and in one way it is – but there is so much more to it. It lends itself to creativity as well and therefore can appeal to a wide range of people with very different skills and interests. Your choice as an ICT teacher is whether to provide education which is broad and covers most of the areas of ICT, or to specialize, or allow your pupils to narrow their focus. Key Stage 4 qualifications are available in general ICT, to help pupils be better users of ICT, and then there are more specific qualifications which may focus on the technical side or on multimedia and the more creative areas. There are even qualifications for post-16 pupils specifically designed to give them the skills to go into particular career paths, such as technical support or web design.

Other subjects have to deal with having a class of pupils where some like the subject and some don't. ICT teachers can often be dealing with three types of pupils: those who like the technical side, those who like the creative side, and the inevitable few who don't like ICT at all.

Are there really pupils who don't like ICT? As I said in the Introduction, whenever I say that I teach ICT I am usually greeted with the comment, 'I bet all the pupils like your subject.' The truth is that a large proportion of pupils do like using computers. Half of the battle is already won – they think positively about the main core of your subject. But the other half of the battle is very difficult as it can seem to the pupils like you are taking something they enjoy and making it boring and hard work. I have had pupils announce firmly in my lessons that they hate computers (usually in a moment of frustration) and then at lunchtime they will be glued to the screen playing a game or checking their emails.

Inevitably there will be pupils in your classes who genuinely don't like

ICT, and that's fine. The world would be a very boring place if we all liked the same things. However, we have a duty to prepare our pupils for the world after school (and even inside school) and therefore they need to be able to use a computer competently to be part of the modern world. Your pupils who don't like the subject will therefore have to at least try – I don't like ironing, but I still have to do it to look smart! Explain to this kind of pupil why it is important that they learn to use a computer well, that whatever job they want to do in the future they will need to use a computer, and that in their personal lives their friends will expect them to use a computer to keep in touch. Even if you have to rationalize with this kind of pupil every lesson and repeat explanations of why ICT is important, keep doing it as eventually they will come over to your way of thinking. Please never resort to 'Because I'm the teacher, and I say so', no matter how irritating the questions or refusals are. Try reasoning with them: 'Look at Barney over there. I know he isn't keen on ICT but look how well he is doing because he is trying and giving it a go.' Or, 'I bet even [insert the name of popular celebrity] knows how to use a computer and has to use it to keep in touch with people.' You could try pairing them up with someone else who is not keen on ICT but is willing to give it a go – don't pair them up with someone who really likes ICT as they will both just find it frustrating. A carrot-and-stick approach may be the best solution: the carrot being something they want, e.g. 'If you finish that whole task, you can go five minutes early' (offer this to the whole class to keep it fair); the stick could be a reminder that the pupil needs to attain a certain level or complete a qualification in the subject – a positive 'stick' rather than a threatening one invoking punishments.

Because ICT is such a wide-ranging subject it is inevitable that some pupils like some areas and other pupils like other areas. Try to combine the two sides of ICT to maximize interest – allow some creativity into the technical side and vice versa. For example, for pupils making a spreadsheet, once they have the correct formulae encourage them to use colours in the cells, change the font and add pictures. For pupils building websites, encourage those who are less keen on the creative aspect to focus on the more mathematical parts, such as proportions of a table to hold the content and whether they should use pixels or percentages.

Some pupils who say they don't like the subject will only be saying that because they find it difficult. If you have tried a pupil on different elements of ICT and they still say they don't like it, or if you notice they complete their tasks more slowly than others in the class, then it may be there is a different issue rather than them just not liking it.

Consider the mobility of the pupil. Might they be having difficulty manipulating the mouse or keyboard? Might there be hand–eye co-ordination issues which have been hidden or not noticed before? Some software requires the user to be very accurate when selecting icons – are they getting frustrated by selecting the wrong icons? If you suspect this may be the case, speak to your SENCO (special educational needs co-ordinator) or someone in the pupil support team who will be able to advise you on how best to support the pupil. It may be that the school, and even the pupil, have been unaware of this problem until now.

Do you know if the pupil has a computer at home? Perhaps the issue could be that they are less experienced than other pupils in using a computer. Whereas others may use them in their own time, this pupil may only use them in your lessons and therefore the process of using a computer is not as natural as we may think it is with most children, being 'digital natives'. On meeting a class for the first time, you may wish to give your classes a quick questionnaire to find out how many pupils do have computers at home, so that you know whether to set computer-based homework, or whether to give only written homework (see this book's companion website for a downloadable example). If you find that a pupil is struggling because they do not have access to a computer at home, you might try to encourage them to use computers in their free time at school. There are also schemes of which you may want to make them or their parents/guardians aware that provide or help with the purchase of a computer with the aim of all school pupils having access to a computer at home.

ICT can be liberating, especially for weak pupils. It can allow those who are weak in certain areas to be supported, without needing another person with them. Typing the words can help those who struggle to move their thoughts and ideas from their heads onto paper. There is a different process that happens when a person types, as opposed to writing by hand. Also, for those with poor handwriting computers can make their words legible. There is an argument against this – that a pupil will never learn to write clearly if they don't practise – but how many adults do you know who have unclear handwriting and are still able to function perfectly well in the world and even be very successful? Doctors, one of the most revered groups of professionals there are, have a reputation for having bad hand-writing. Think about how much you write by hand now and how much you type into a computer. I find that the only things I write by hand are the things that only I have to read. A computer can support not only the use of English, but also the use of maths, with the provision of calculators and spreadsheets. I do my household budget using a spreadsheet because it is reduces the possibility of making an error if I just did it on paper. We should no longer be debating whether computers and calculators should be used in Maths, but how to use them well, because in the real world our pupils will always have access to a calculator – they carry one in their pockets on their mobile phones. Research is so much easier with the advent of the internet, all the information one person could ever want (and some they don't want) is just a click away. If a pupil doesn't know something, it can be easily resolved, as long as they have a computer to be able to look it up on. It could be argued that it is now a more important skill to know how to find out information than to actually know information. Generally when a pupil has looked up and found the information themselves they remember it better than just being told it.

ICT can also be empowering for SEN pupils, those with physical disabilities and learning difficulties. Without any modifications being made, computers can help with skills such as reading by allowing writing to be made larger at the click of a button or the font and the colour of the background to be changed. With the addition of specialist software, they can provide assistance like reading text from a document or web page. Extra peripherals can be purchased, everything from a trackball mouse, which is quite common, to specialized input devices, floor turtles and multi-sensory environments. ICT can give pupils greater independence and a greater sense of achievement. If you want to read further on this topic, an excellent book is *Dyslexia in the Digital Age* by Ian Smythe.

Computers can provide an uncluttered environment and encourage focus, but we sometimes think of computers as confusing environments, with many things happening at once. The easily distracted can be lured into email-checking and internet surfing. However, if they are set up in a certain way, computers can focus thinking and learning by only giving access to the elements which are needed. This can be useful for pupils who do find it difficult to concentrate. And if previously distracted pupils complete the set work well, perhaps they can have the last ten minutes of the lesson surfing the internet or checking their email with the environment unblocked as a reward.

ICT provides a non-judgemental, non-threatening environment in which students can try out their ideas. Unlike putting their hand up and answering a question in class, pupils can answer a question on the computer without fear of failure in front of their classmates and teacher, or being branded a 'swot' by knowing all of the answers. It is a tool which unshackles pupils from prejudice and encourages trial and error, learning through play, and also gives them the freedom to learn independently.

Extended independent projects

There is the opportunity in ICT to give pupils larger projects to work on. No matter what their age, they will enjoy taking ownership of a task and being responsible for its successful completion. It is key that the instructions are very clear and should include what the finished product should be, what the time limit is, the resources which can be used, who the people involved are, where they can find help, and any things they must or must not do during the project. Once the parameters are set they then have freedom within them to create their own product.

Usually a project like this would take place across a few lessons (or a couple of weeks). Any shorter and there may not be time to complete a substantial, meaningful project; any longer and pupils may become distracted or lose interest. If the project will take a long time due to its size, consider breaking it into smaller chunks which are either assessed at stages by yourself or by the pupils themselves.

This type of project would generally be done in teams and could either be part of their ICT education or something extra-curricular. It could even become a competition, with the winning product being the one which is used (examples might be a page on the school's VLE or in the school magazine, or a resource to be used in class). You could get an outside 'client' involved and the pupils could make something for a local business or event which is about to take place.

○━ A lot of these extended, independent projects will be creative ones, just by the nature of the tasks involved. It may be to produce a presentation, a website, a poster – or even a set of these products on one topic. How do you encourage creativity? You may have pupils in your class who leap at the chance of being creative and they will be fine with a brief that allows them to use their imagination and come up with ideas. There will also be other pupils who are not good in this area and there may be two reasons for that: a) they are genuinely not very good at coming up with new ideas; or b) they have been stifled or knocked back in the past and don't have the confidence to disclose their ideas. Make sure you have thought about the project beforehand as you may need to give some leading suggestions as to possible ways to tackle the project. For example, in putting together a presentation, you may suggest to a team which is struggling to think of something original something like: 'Do you really need to use PowerPoint? I've got some cameras you could use . . . ' Don't tell them what to do, as this defeats the object of letting them have an open brief, but just suggest enough to get them started. Hopefully once you do, they will jump on the idea and run with it. Just because some pupils are not good at coming up with ideas, it does not mean they are unable to carry out ideas creatively. With those who seem reticent about sharing their ideas, perhaps sit with the group and spend 5 minutes telling them there is no such thing as a bad idea and praising every idea that comes out. Alternatively, give them big sheets of paper and marker pens and tell them to cover the sheet in as many ideas as possible in 30 seconds. When the time is up the sheet should be littered with all sorts of ideas and it will not be known whose is whose.

If you want your pupils to be very creative, you may wish to do a starter activity to get them thinking creatively, or even give them a whole lesson on creativity before the start of the project (see this book's companion website for ideas for activities using creativity).

By doing these types of extended projects pupils will develop not only their ICT skills but other very important skills as well, such as:

- group work
- communication
- planning
- time management
- organization
- independence in learning
- problem-solving.

These skills are the vital, transferable ones which are so sought after by higher education and employers. Projects like these give pupils a chance to develop these skills and allow them to give an example on application forms of where they have used them.

By handing over the responsibility to the pupils, they get a much richer experience and develop a wider range of skills. However, it can be difficult for the teacher to be hands-off. Teachers generally like to be in control – it is one of the skills that is very important in teaching and something that a lot of us do well. Relinquishing control can be scary. There may be a fear that complete chaos will ensue if we give up our control, that as soon as we take our hand off the tiller the boat will hit a storm and be buffeted all over. Or worse, that if we are not steering it forwards inertia will take over and our boat will just bob on the big expanse of ocean and nothing will happen. There is a certain amount of risk involved in handing responsibility to your pupils, and I wouldn't suggest you do it for the first time during an important project such as coursework – perhaps introduce it to a younger group. I have never yet seen pupils not step up to the mark when they are trusted with their own project. They really enjoy it, especially if it is something they have not experienced before. As long as the parameters are set and they can work within a defined area and time-frame, you will hopefully be pleasantly surprised about the final product they produce and the energy and enthusiasm they put into the project. You may find pupils who have never shown an interest in ICT really being motivated because they now have the control. The difficult thing for you is to remain hands-off. You will see them heading towards mistakes and problems, but you have to let them encounter those problems, because if they don't experience them they will never learn how to fix them. Learning from mistakes is a vital part of growing up and one which seems to be somewhat discouraged these days in education. The emphasis is on always getting it right, and students are never given the time to fail and learn the valuable lesson of picking themselves back up and trying again. Obviously if you see them heading towards something dangerous, such as thinking their poster would benefit from having photographs from a building site, then step in and stop them, but otherwise allow them to make the mistakes. It will be difficult not to step in, but they will benefit from facing the difficulties, or even by not completing the project at all. Failure is a positive lesson, especially if you spin it as a positive – that is the point you can step in and reassure them with. Remember, even though you are going to hand over responsibility, you can always step in if you see that you need to make a change and you will be monitoring what is happening. Perhaps a new parameter will be needed part way through the project, if you see all the groups heading in the wrong direction or you realize there is a loophole. Announce it as though you were always going to throw in a curveball at this point and pose it as a challenge, e.g. 'You are doing really well with your animations and I said they had to be longer than one minute – well here's another challenge: they must be less than five minutes!' – this will stop them creating something mammoth which you'll know from experience they will not have time to complete.

Ambition is good, but sometimes pupils can over-reach and you need to bring them back a little, being careful not to suppress their enthusiasm.

○━ Never let pupils know that you are winging it! There are times when all teachers have to make it up as they go along, and that is part of the excitement of the job. You never really know what pupils will do and what you may think is a well-prepared activity that can only be done in one way may produce surprising results once real pupils try it out. Experience gives you more skill in judging what pupils may do and where the ambiguities may be, but even so young people often see things quite differently to us. But that is a great part of the job.

Teaching flexibly is actually a positive skill, as long as you don't rely on it. Never walk into a classroom having not at least thought about what you will do and if possible never walk in without having prepared the lesson. However, if you have a thorough plan and always stick to it, no matter what is actually happening in the lesson, you may miss out on opportunities to further the pupils' knowledge or to get them more motivated and involved in a task. For example, if you are having a class discussion about e-commerce and suddenly a pupil makes a comment about privacy and the others seem really keen to discuss it, allow some time for them to explore this idea. As long as your learning objectives are met by the end of the lesson, or can be achieved in the following lesson, then there is no problem in permitting a small deviation in topic. It is your skill in managing a situation and forward planning that will allow you to do this – manage the conversation and bring it back around to the original topic again and know what the following lessons will be and whether you can use this.

Getting girls into ICT

Although ICT is becoming more open to girls, there is still a disproportionately low number of girls taking it forward for a career. Girls tend to be more willing to sit courses which are aimed at them becoming users of ICT, rather than experts. Even if they do choose ICT as part of their education, their achievement on the whole in the subject is not as high as the boys sitting the same courses. There is still the stereotype in ICT of a geeky boy sat in his bedroom tinkering away with computer components and coding, and girls can have difficulty identifying ICT as an opportunity for them.

In reality, there is real demand for women in ICT, to the point where there are special groups set up all over the country to encourage women into ICT, such as GirlGeeks, and some companies are specifically targeting women for employment. Games design companies are eager to get more women into their teams – they know women gamers are a large and growing part of their market, but with design teams being mostly male they are concerned about lacking the female perspective to guide them into designing games for this potentially lucrative market. Girls can feel threatened by being in the minority. I remember walking into a new class on artificial intelligence at university and being confronted by a whole room of young men and, as I took my seat by myself, I was interested to see the lecturer as *she* walked in. It had been an issue that I hadn't really thought about previously, but that feeling of being in the minority stayed with me and I can understand why there is a perceived barrier to women in ICT.

Many girls may only see men being ICT practitioners: her ICT teacher might be male, the technicians in the school might all be males and at home her father might use a computer for his work which her mother does not use very much. Subconsciously she may have associated computers with men and may not consider it something which she can get into or something that could be part of her life. Now I'm not suggesting that if you are a male ICT teacher you should rush off and get a sex change! Neither am I suggesting that a female ICT teacher should be hired over a male, because it should always be the best person for the job. However, if you are aware that the girls in your school are surrounded by male role models in ICT, consider inviting a female teacher of another subject who is interested in ICT to teach a little bit of ICT. Perhaps you could do a swap and teach her subject for a few lessons. Alternatively, you might want to invite a female speaker to talk to your pupils about ICT. Don't make it obvious that you have sought out a female to talk about ICT, because that will defeat the object of your pupils, both female and male, understanding that it is normal to have people of both genders working in the field.

It should be made clear at this point that the disparity between males and females studying ICT is lessening and is much better than it used to be – it is still an issue, however. Just like there are campaigns devoted to getting more girls into Science and Maths, girls need to be encouraged into ICT. There have been more girls going into the field of multimedia as that has become more popular, but there is still no reason why we shouldn't have more girls studying 'harder' areas of ICT such as networking and programming.

Recently Barbie was given her 125th career since her release in 1959. Her latest career move was to become a computer engineer. Interestingly, this was also the first time the public have voted on a career for Barbie. In a press release, Mattel explained that Barbie, who is 'always a trailblazer . . . inspires a new generation of girls to explore this importantly high-tech industry, which continues to grow and need future female leaders'. Computer Engineer Barbie comes with a computer-themed T-shirt and black trousers, pink glasses, a Bluetooth headset, a smartphone and a pink laptop. There have been mixed reactions. On the one hand the response has been positive, with the hope that this new Barbie will demonstrate to young girls that a career in computing is open to them and that they will not think it an unusual direction – if Barbie can do it, any girl can do it. Having Barbie as an intelligent role model may be better than her posing in bikinis. On the other hand there is the worry that Barbie is only furthering the stereotype that all geeks wear glasses, wear binary on their clothes and walk around with headsets on.

Getting girls excited about ICT is going to take more than colouring things in pink! Although it may attract some, it is actually sending an even more stereotyped message: 'Here girls, you use this technology because it's in your special colour.' Also, don't think that making the topic 'girly' will work either. Making a database about dolls or celebrity weddings is going to alienate not only the majority of your girls further but your boys as well. If you look in older textbooks, those which have thankfully been superseded, they use examples which are stereotypically male interests such as football, cars or even wrestling (it did have to be explained to me that the WWF referred to in the question was not the World Wildlife Fund). Of course, there are girls who are interested in these areas, but they are less likely to capture the imaginations of the majority of them.

In order to have less gender-specific examples, consider things that are done by both girls and boys, such as eating, wearing clothes and making friends. Interesting projects could include finding out the nutrition in fast food, researching fashions from different times and cultures, or gathering information from their friends about their interests or opinions. Both girls and boys can get interested about issues such as the environment, health, culture or new scientific discoveries. The key thing is to make ICT relevant, valuable and useful – if it becomes frivolous or pointless then you will lose the interest of both genders in your class.

You could also consider the introduction of extra-curricular groups focused on ICT for girls. Perhaps you could pass responsibility to some of your girls and encourage them, with your support, to set up a group for other girls to join and take part in ICT projects.

Overall it must be remembered that girls are not a special subset of your pupils – they have an equal right to education in ICT as boys, just as the boys should not be forgotten in your pursuit of getting girls involved. The barriers must be overcome while promoting ICT to both genders.

Digital natives and digital immigrants

In his 2001 book, *Digital Game-based Learning*, Marc Prensky coined the terms 'digital natives' and 'digital immigrants' to refer to those who were born into the digital age and those who were not; those who are completely at home in modern society and using the technology of the day, and those to whom it is more alien.

There is gap of at least one generation between teachers and pupils and this will always be the case. However, the present gap is more obvious because the introduction of ICT and its increasing availability and capability has made it more pronounced.

Today's pupils did not experience a time without the internet and mobile phones, without computers being the norm or televisions with more channels than you could ever want. They are the digital natives, they are the indigenous inhabitants of this place.

Today's teachers, on the other hand, can remember what it was like without the internet, when to find out information you had to look in a book, visit a library, read a newspaper or listen to the radio. Some teachers will remember when their homes had their first dial-up internet line installed, unlike their pupils, who may believe homes have always had high-speed broadband. Teachers will remember payphones and being completely unreachable, whereas pupils can use their mobile phones not only to make calls anywhere but also to send messages, images or even surf the internet; they are never disconnected.

Digital natives work and use computers in a different way to digital immigrants. The most obvious difference between them, which you will probably have seen, is the level of multi-tasking they are capable of. Unlike older users, who usually have one thing on their screen at a time, natives will often be running several programs at once: a document they are writing, a browser window looking up information, a chat screen talking to their friends, and so on. Their screens may appear cluttered and chaotic, and yet they will be able to manage this space and work on several things simultaneously. I once asked a pupil in my class why he couldn't concentrate on a piece of work and he replied, 'Because you make us do one thing at a time and I get distracted.' As a digital native, he was used to multi-tasking and being asked to do one thing at a time in class left him open to other diversions. I overcame this by handing out two tasks at a time and let the pupils decide if they wanted to do the first one, then the second one, or flit between the two – as long as they completed them both, they could have control over exactly how they would do it.

Another area you may see digital natives being out of their depth in is a library. Most schools have libraries and their pupils are taught library skills: how to find a book, how to look in the index, etc. Do young people need to know this? Are traditional libraries something we should have in schools or should we be looking to upgrade them to more modern, relevant spaces? When pupils are shown their school's library and how it works, their first question is often either, 'Why do I need books when I can look it up on the internet?' or 'Where are the computers?' I often see teachers and librarians become very frustrated at these questions – how dare these young people question the need for books?! However, in our digital age, as many books are being transferred onto computer anyway, is a room of books still a valuable provision in a school? Is it not true that, although older people may find these places warm, inviting and reassuring, young people find such places cold, dull, old-fashioned and alien? To them, words appear in pixels, not print. If they are digital natives and we the digital immigrants, are we not the literary natives and they the literary immigrants? This process goes both ways, and what we are familiar with they can find abnormal, perplexing and incongruous. I am not advocating the removal of libraries – certainly not. However, it should be considered that they could be converted into spaces that both digital natives and immigrants can understand and enjoy. If a school library is turned into a learning-resource centre, not only can both pupils and staff enjoy the space and facilities, but a place such as this can become the hub of the school, a central point that is visited regularly and becomes integral. By combining the old and the new, books and computers, tables to write at and power sockets for laptops, open areas for collaborative working and booths for individual work, the traditional library can become a flexible area which can be used for more types of activity than just reading books or working with pen and paper.

It has been said that we now live in a world where sound bites carry more weight than speeches. Although this scenario has been created by the media, it is the world that digital natives are used to – why would they read a whole article when all they need are the key facts? Giving pupils large pieces of reading will be something with which they are not used to and, although for some subjects developing this skill is a necessary, it is not something which will come naturally to the young people of today.

In addition, we live in an AV culture, where we receive audio-visual stimulus all the time. Even just walking down the street in our nearest town or city we are greeted with digital signage, computerized billboards, recorded music, announcements, flashy animations, eye-catching imagery and other technology being used wherever and whenever possible. Although to us this may seem new and remarkable, to young people it is the norm, something which has always been there and, possibly unlike us, something which they can tune in and out of as they need. Whereas older people may walk down the street with their attention being caught by every animated sign they see, young people may not even notice the signs are there. Consider television programmes as well, especially those made for children and teenagers – they jump from topic to topic, only spending a few minutes on one thing before moving to the next. These are the paradigms in which they are growing up and which they find exciting and keep their attention. The way films for young people are made also uses this change in attention spans: whereas older films would often include long scenes of dialogue and static camera shots, modern films are cut and edited in order to appeal to the audience's attention spans. Research by the University of Texas found that an actual formula could be applied to films, mostly after 1990, to find a pattern in the editing of the film's shots. Therefore, if their experience in the classroom is different to the whizz-bang nature of their 'normal' lives, they may tend to find it boring and even extraordinary; they go to school and it is so different from the rest of their lives that it may seem not part of their lives, or not important because it is so different.

Young people also live in a world where collaborative working is arguably more important that individual working. Although the individual is still important and independent thought is vital, being able to work in a team is essential to function in the modern world. Yet school systems are geared to assessing individuals and almost push education away from group work, especially for pupils working towards qualifications. Once a pupil reaches about the age of 14, they are often compelled to mostly work individually. This is mainly for reasons of assessment, and exam boards, for most of their qualifications, will not allow group work or collaborative work to be submitted. It is understandable, as assessing group work is difficult and allocating individual grades based on it can become a nightmare when you have to justify it. However, digital natives are used to collaborating and it is a more natural way for them to work; in fact to them it makes more sense – if they cannot do something, they find the person who can. That person may not necessarily be a teacher because, in this age of 24/7, teachers are not available at 11 p.m. when they may be doing their homework. It is therefore easy to appreciate that when school forces young people to work individually they often find it hard to resist working with others, and what teachers may interpret as copying or getting another pupil to do the work for them is in fact pupils working together, as comes naturally to them.

Just because modern young people work in a different way to us does not mean their way is wrong or that they are learning less efficiently. In fact, they are developing skills for their modern world, just like we developed skills for ours which are perhaps no longer as important. I know exactly how the Dewey decimal system works – but as I mostly look things up on the internet, is that a useful skill for this age?

We need to acknowledge that today's young people learn in a different way to us and need a different skill set to take their place in the modern world. If schools don't 'move with the times' then they will become relics, a reminiscence of a bygone era and things in which young people will become increasingly dissatisfied. I propose that it is partly this that is causing some of the problems in schools, including behaviour, absenteeism and low achievement. Imagine you are given a task to do and told you have to do it – if you think it is not valuable or old-fashioned (and you could think of a better way to do it), how much effort would you really put into it? If you are asked to do something that you are told will benefit you, but you can't see how, are you really going to do it to the best of your ability? Or will you do the minimum so you can move on to something more relevant and exciting?

As teachers, we can make a big difference in this area. We can acknowledge the new ways in which our young people can and like to learn, and draw on these in order to make our lessons increasingly engaging, significant and worthwhile. We can ensure that our pupils understand why they are learning specific topics and show them the value of what we are doing together – them and us working as a partnership rather than two warring sides.

There are also changes which could be made on a bigger scale: at department level, school level, by exam boards and the government. It needs to be understood by the digital immigrants who are deciding what young people learn and how they learn it that they are dealing with digital natives – that the world that they will inhabit after their education is very different to the one which digital immigrants have been living in for 30, 50, 60 years. Although teachers do have immediate power over their pupils, they can only operate within the parameters given to them.

If an exam board will only allow individual assessment for a qualification, then pupils sitting that course will never be assessed on their teamworking skills, and yet I can virtually guarantee that every job these young people will apply for will expect them to have these skills.

We must recognize that our young people, and those yet to join our schools, live in a new, digital age. We must ensure we approach their learning, their experience of education, with this in mind and, rather than ignoring or dismissing it, use it to our advantage. It is much easier, and proves to be more valuable to all concerned, if you utilize their already existing way of working in order to produce the desired results. Engage with them, find out what makes them tick, use topics that they connect with, chat to them about their interests – treat them as people and as individuals. This is not 'if you can't beat them, join them'; this is the understanding that the new world is their world and we must prepare them for it, as surely that is the object of education.

The Future

Young people nowadays have their eye on the prize much earlier than previous generations. 'What do you want to be when you grow up?' is a question which comes into their consciousness much earlier and, whereas once the answer given might have been aspirational, today it increasingly requires a more realistic response. Children are very aware that the world of work is different to that of their parents' and grandparents' generations. They know they will not stay in one job for life; they know that they may not be expected to follow the path their parents took; and they know that there are pressures of employment and finances and families – they are more aware of what adult life may be like when they reach it, even if they don't acknowledge it. However, they also know that they live in an exciting time of opportunity. Girls and boys, the women and men of the future, can look forward to a life of choice, of opportunity, of empowerment. More than ever before there are chances and possibilities open to our young people.

My family history, only two generations back, is of living in a small village where the men worked down the coal mine and the women stayed at home and looked after the men and the children. The furthest they ever travelled was to the nearest city 4 miles away or to the nearest coastal town for a rare short holiday. One generation back, both of my parents worked full-time, each in a career that was very different to that of their parents – my dad went to art college (a very radical thing at the time) and stayed with the same company for 35 years. They own their own car and their own house and have travelled around the UK and to Europe. In my generation, I had the opportunity to go to university, the first member of my immediate family, and it was more a natural progression than something I had to fight for. I chose to become a teacher and was able to make that decision freely, based on where my skills lay and what I wanted to do. I know I will have several job changes over my career, even in the relatively secure environment of education. I think nothing of driving for 2 or 3 hours to get to where I want to go and whizzing round the country to conferences and other events. I travel abroad, but still think of it as exotic and unusual.

The next generation, the young people I teach, have boundless opportunities open to them, the freedom to experience as much education as they would like and are encouraged to do so with financial incentives. The only limitations are their own ability and willingness. They may have ten to fifteen jobs over their lifetime, they may have to change careers several times, they may need to learn skills that we can't even foresee yet. They may live in a world that we can't even imagine, much less prepare them for. They may own their own car, they may have two – they may have ones which run on biofuel, talk to them and even hover above the road! They will think nothing of international travel and see the world as a small place – no matter where they go in it they will still be connected to the rest of it. They will have networks of people, friends, associates whom they have never met yet may still know intimately.

They have the whole world and every opportunity open to them. We, as educators, mentors and guides, have to help them navigate this huge wealth of possibility. We have to show them that they can truly do anything, be anything they want to be, and that no dream is too big or too small. As you stand in your classroom, looking at your pupils, just think what tremendous things each one of them is capable of doing and that each one of them can change the world. We must believe in our young people, support them; just like we would help a baby stand up and take its first steps, we must help them to take their first steps into adulthood and give them the tools, knowledge, experiences and confidence to take their place in the world. We must show them how to make a positive contribution to society, how to be interesting and informed people, and show them that they all have the chance to be happy and important people.

No matter how hard the job of teaching can get, remember that you are doing one of the most important jobs in the world and that you are creating the next generation who will shape the world.

Never forget that above all you are a teacher and it's the best job in the world!

Index